Expected Hope

Written by:
Steven Crutchfield

Cadmus Publishing
www.cadmuspublishing.com

ACKNOWLEDGEMENT TO:

Donna Inanen for loving me and other incarcerated men and women unconditionally. Thank you for putting up with me, enabling me to make this dream happen, for partnering with me in this mission.

DEDICATED TO:

God my Father and His Son Jesus Christ who has blessed me in more ways than I could have ever imagined.

Dawn Marie, Steven Zachery, Joshua Allen and Meagan Marie (Nicole). Though I was not the husband and father you deserved, you are and will always be my inspiration. I love you!

Michael Sasso. Your death was not in vain. I have lived every day in and for your memory, to affect positive, life changing decisions for myself and many other incarcerated men and women. You changed many lives!

CONTENTS

INTRODUCTION

G reat calamity shall come upon your life. Fear not. It is not unto death." These words startled me out of my prayer. It was such a straightforward statement of fact. I shrugged it off as this could mean many things. My desire was to be a medical doctor, more specifically a medical missionary to Mali, West Africa. I attended college studying a double major in microbiology and chemistry. While the declarative statement resonated deep in my spirit it did not cause me any anxiety or worry. "Great calamity" could be financial in nature, sickness, or a myriad of other trials and tribulations. Yet, I knew one thing was for certain, ". . . He will never leave me or forsake me (Hebrews 13:5)."

Five years earlier two men of God, my "Promise Keeper's" mentors, approached me and began explaining that God wanted me to begin a prison ministry at the medium security facility in Danville, Illinois.

Now, just a little back story. I was born and raised in Texas. Justice to me was, "Don't put 'em in prison, bury 'em under the prison." I could see the utter shock on those two men's faces as I loudly exclaimed, "Hell no! Those convicts, felons, and criminals had the chance to know God and accept Jesus on the streets as free men but rejected them. They've got nothing coming from me."

On the ride home from church that morning I explained the encounter to my wife. With righteous indignation I rationalized how they had to be wrong because God had specifically called me to be a "healer." It was clear, at least in my mind, that God was calling me into the noble profession of medical arts. I welcomed the physical, emotional, and intellectual challenges that lie ahead. However, I became unsettled when my wife neither agreed with me nor disagreed with them.

Soon after arriving home, we sat down for our Sunday lunch when the telephone rang. I answered it only to hear an automated message, "You have a collect call from . . . an inmate in the Illinois Department of Corrections, Danville." Furious that an inmate had my home telephone number, I hung up and called the Danville prison to explain my concern as neither my wife nor I was acquainted with anyone serving time in prison. The person on the other end of the line assured me that the matter would be handled swiftly and punishment meted out if warranted.

As far as I was concerned, it was warranted. There was no reason for a convicted felon to have our telephone number, let alone try to communicate with us. Retributive justice for an attempted telephone call? Absolutely! Scumbag inmates did not even deserve access to a telephone.

Unfortunately, this I what I truly believed. This is what had been taught to me growing up in Texas. When I began attending my church my freshman year in high school, this was the same attitude preached from the pulpits. The pastors would preach "love" but in the same sermon provide a scathing discourse about the godless homosexual, HIV/AIDS patients, and convicts. These people were all effectively unlovable. I sat there offering my "Amen" and "Praise the Lord." I was fully immersed in and indoctrinated into these beliefs for many years.

Looking back now I recognize I was in bondage to this doctrine of the unlovable. How wrong I was. As I pen this book from my prison cell, I now see clearly how easy it is to love your family, friends, and those people sitting in the pews. It is easy to love those who are likeminded. Yet, it is terribly difficult to wholeheartedly follow the command:

"A new commandment I give unto you, that you love one another; as I have loved you, that you also love one another. By this shall all men know that you are My disciples, if you have love for one another."
- John 13:34-35

Ask yourself, is it difficult for me to love those that society has deemed unlovable and discarded as rubbish on the trash heap of life? The homeless? The inmate? The HIV/AIDS patient? The homosexual? The woman who had an abortion?

I never knew the meaning of "love the sinner but hate the sin." As I was taught, the sin and the sinner were one and the same. These unlovable societal rejects were to be shunned in a sense. If they wanted to repent and accept Christ, good. If not, we were not to have anything to do with them. Even if they did accept Christ, their previous lifestyle and choices prevented their full acceptance. As one pastor so bluntly put it, "Good luck, hell is a hot place."

What is love? To me, it was loving those who loved me. My mother rejected me, no love for her. My father rejected me, no love for him, either. This thinking was contrary to the commandment to "honor your father and mother (Exodus 20:12)." There was so much for me to learn but there was so much more to be unlearned.

CHAPTER 1

"Therefore my people are gone into captivity, because they have no knowledge …" - Isaiah 5:13

April 4, 1999 remains to this day a shrouded mystery. I believe God supernaturally covered my mind to protect me from the events that occurred. I can recite the testimony provided of those events, yet I have no personal memory of the crime for which I was to be charged.

The metal handcuffs bit smartly into my wrists. Where am I? What time is it? Why am I being arrested? The arresting officer was unwilling to answer any of my questions but was quick to read me my Miranda rights. At the county jail I was notified that I was under arrest for the murder of my wife's lover. How could this be? I sobbed deeply. It was not for my wife. It was not for the destruction of my marriage or the loss of my children. It was because I was accused of causing the death of another person. This was an unbearable thought. I could not live with the thought of being the cause of someone losing their life. Such shame, humiliation, and condemnation burdened me to the point that I began praying for death. I was walking headlong *"into the valley of the shadow of death (Psalm 23:4),"* and death was stalking me as its prey.

I was booked into the county jail, fingerprinted, photo-graphed, strip-searched, showered, and deloused. Each new arrival was given one towel, one blanket, a toothbrush, sample size toothpaste and soap, a drinking cup, and a blaze orange jumpsuit with a pair of blaze orange shower shoes. My life was reduced to what could fit in a brown paper bag.

My first day in jail was met with confusion, anxiety and an-ger. I knew only one thing from watching prison television shows: someone would always try the new guy. I guess my case was no different. When lunch came a "chuck-hole" was opened and each man stood waiting to take his own drink and tray of food that was shoved through the opening. Awaiting my turn, a man gruffly said, "You ain't eating. I'm eating your tray." My first instinct was a sense of fear rising up but I stifled that quickly knowing fear was a weakness to be exploited. I had never feared anyone or anything in my life and I was not about to start now. Here it was, I was being tried by a much larger man for the right to eat of all things – jail food. Come on!

I quickly calculated in my mind five different scenarios and outcomes.

1. He would beat me, eat my food, and continue to be a bully.

2. I would beat him, eat both trays of food.

3. He would kill me.

4. I would kill him.

5. He would back down.

My tray of food appeared and I grabbed it along with my cup of juice. Stepping to the side, I waited for the man. The tension was palpable and the other men were waiting to see the outcome.

As the other man took his tray and stepped toward me, I

glared at him with these crazy eyes I get when angered and offered him my food with this caveat: "If you take this tray of food I will kill you." The tone was set and the gauntlet thrown down. He laughed and this enraged me all the more. Admittedly, I have a bully-complex and despise bullies. Handing him the tray I looked toward heaven and said loudly in my best maniacal voice, "I thank you for this sacrifice you have provided for me. May his blood and his body be received as I offer him up to you with joy."

No one was eating now, only staring. The man was visibly nervous but did not know how to extricate himself from the situation. I kept offering him the tray, calling him "sacrifice." Take the tray you *#x!-ing sacrifice." I was charged with internal rage. He refused to take the tray so I shoved it into his chest yelling, "You are the chosen sacrifice." Finally, he simply walked away nervously exclaiming, "Man, I was just kidding with you." Later, I learned he did this to every new person who entered the block. That ended the day I moved in.

A few days later a former co-worker and friend who had retained some of my belongings had sent me my Ryrie Study Bible. When I received it, I became very emotional. It was as if I was meeting a long lost love. Once you thought that flame of love was dead, but the smallest glow of an ember signifies that there is still something to that love. Receiving that Bible sparked a flame of love in me that saved my life – I thought!

"Doc, you have court this morning," came the bellow from the cellblock door. This was confusing as I had learned in the previous weeks of my incarceration that you were always notified by mail of any upcoming court dates requiring your appearance. I exited the cellblock into the hall where I was patted down and required to wear ankle shackles, handcuffs and a belly chain wrapped around my waist. The handcuffs and ankle shackles were secured to the belly chain. This was an odd turn of events as I had never been shackled like this before in previous court appearances.

Entering the courtroom, there was complete silence. The tension was ominous. The only sound was that of the chains clinking as I shuffled to a pre-determined seat between my two public defenders. My attorneys did not greet or even acknowledge me. I certainly did not like the vibe I was getting.

"All rise," came the bailiff's call as the judge entered the courtroom and sat in his elevated position looking down on the rest of the court. "Be seated. We're on the record. Let the record reflect that the state's attorney is present, the defendant is present as are the defendant's attorneys. State, are you ready to proceed?"

"Yes, your honor. The state files and serves notice to the court and the defendant that it will seek the death penalty."

A crushing feeling overwhelmed me, my breath literally taken away. The hearing was a formality that lasted less than two minutes. Notice was duly served that the state of Illinois was going to seek my execution. The walk back to the elevator and the ride back up to the jail was silent and somber. I made my way back to my cell, hung my curtain for a little privacy, and wept silently. I wanted to pray but the only words I could speak were, "My Lord, why have you forsaken me?" Later, I emerged from my cell and explained to the guys my new situation. They already knew. While I was in court, the morning T.V. news was reporting the story.

Later that same day I received a message to call my grandmother at the number she provided. I had not seen or heard from her since my mother's funeral nine years earlier. Immediately I called the number. The very first words spoken to me by my grandmother in nine years was, "Steve, if you get the death penalty, can we be the witnesses?" Devastated, I hung up the phone.

Once again, I returned to my cell, hung my curtain for a little privacy to pray. This time I heard that same unmistakable voice in my spirit, "Fear not. It is not unto death." At that moment, I knew that I would live and not die by the executioner's needle.

"And fear not them which kill the body, but are not able to kill the soul: but rather fear Him who is able to destroy both soul and body in hell."
— Matthew 10:28

I did not know what the future held for me but I would face it with confident assurance that sovereign God was in control.

"For which cause I suffer these things: nevertheless I am not ashamed: for I know whom I have believed and am persuaded that He is able to keep that which I have committed unto Him against that day."
II Timothy 1:12

Ten months later I was locked in a holding cell by myself while the jury deliberated. It was actually the "drunk tank" that was used to hold the drunks until they were either sober or could make bond. It was eight by ten with a concrete slab as a bed-stand and a stainless steel sink-toilet combo. The "tank" smelled of years of urine and vomit. It was not routinely cleaned by the jail trustees that were tasked with the job.

Lying on the filthy, paper-thin mattress I began to reflect on the three week trial. Throughout, I prayed desperately, fervently that the jury would recognize the mitigating factor of adultery. I never claimed actual innocence. That would have been preposterous. Truly, I was culpable for the death of the man. I just needed the jury to see that I was less culpable than first degree pre-meditated murder.

The verdict was in. The sheriff's deputy strapped an electronic shocking device to me called a shock box. It would deliver a seven second, fifty-thousand volt jolt of electricity to my body if I acted in an inappropriate manner. As the jury filed in I took notice that they would not look at me. This was a bad sign. I knew enough from watching television court dramas that if the jury came back in the courtroom and avoided eye contact with you, your goose was cooked.

I was convicted of first degree murder. This was so upsetting because my defense was one of a second degree murder crime of passion based on adultery of my spouse. Not only did they find me guilty of the murder they also found me guilty of the aggravating factor of "brutal, heinous, indicative of wanton cruelty." The jury summarily rejected my defense of crime of passion.

It was a devastating blow. The sentencing range for first degree murder in Illinois was twenty to sixty years or up to natural life. I knew the reason the state had requested the special "Apprendi" instruction for the aggravating factor was to ensure I received an extended term sentence. The death penalty had been taken off the table apparently after the family spoke with the state's attorney. God's word was true, it was "not unto death." However, there was no hope of a minimum sentence. Sentencing was scheduled to take place in 90 days, time enough to perform a pre-sentence investigation. This was supposed to dig up all the dirt in your past or to find mitigating factors that could give the judge a reason to mete out a lighter sentence.

Sentencing day came, the day of days. I admit, I spent the previous ninety days in anger and bitterness. I shaved my head and grew a full Osama bin Laden beard. The guys in the cellblock referred to me as Osama bin Doc. My thought was they convicted me and labeled me a heartless stone-cold killer so I would at least look the part. I was dressed in my blaze orange jumpsuit, a pair of white socks and was wearing my blaze orange shower shoes affectionately known as "Jesus Creepers" among the inmates. Once again, I was shackled and manacled at the wrists and ankles, and belly chained.

As I entered the courtroom I noticed my sister, stepsister and stepmother. My attorneys had subpoenaed them to testify at the sentencing hearing on my behalf. Their testimony would be a lie. I knew this and for that reason I did not want my attorneys to have them testify. I had been estranged from my family for several years. Why? I chose a different path in life than what was expected of me. I did not want to live scraping by paycheck to paycheck or living on the government dole. I wanted to be successful. I chose to graduate high school. I chose to enlist in the United States Air Force. I chose to go to college. I chose a career path that required me to work smarter not harder. I did not want to be a laborer.

I purchased my first home at the age of twenty-two. My wife and I had nice clothes, a nice car, and money to spend. Simply put, my family saw me as "uppity." That was okay by me. I just told my wife I was the "white" sheep of the family.

Just as I expected, one by one they got up on the witness stand, swore under oath to tell the truth and nothing but the truth. My only thought was that perjury carries a penalty of up to three years. They testified to stories about me that I never remembered and never happened, extolling the virtues of a good brother and son. They even shed a few tears to make it seem more real. The truth was they had never been to my home, never met my children who by this time were ages seven, five, and three. They never called, sent a single holiday or birthday card and I was never notified of any family reunions. It was difficult to stifle my laughter at the farce being played out before the court where they expressed their undying love for me.

Now it was my turn to address the court. It is called the "right to allocution" where a convicted person has the right to make a final statement. As angry and bitter as I was, I would not speak in open court. I could not in good conscience stand before a judge and beg for mercy while the victim's family sat looking on. No! I had shown no mercy to their son. Therefore, I would not ask for mercy from the family or the judge. I was not entitled to mercy and to beg for it would have been a slap in the face, a disservice to that grieving family. However, I did provide a letter to the judge for his consideration. The full text of the statement reads as follows:

"I have arrived at the crossroads, having to address this honorable court. Unfortunately, words, no matter how well penned or eloquently spoken, cannot suffice to properly convey with all sincerity and with the extreme remorse that I feel. I offer no excuse as there can be no excuse for the taking of a life. I alone accept full responsibility for the crime which I have been convicted of.

My remorse for this act is not and will never be abated and serves as an ever present and ever prevalent reminder of the sorrow, grief, and pain I have caused. For that I offer my sincerest apologies. Prior to trial I wrote the family to express my apology. The reason I will not read this aloud in court is that I do not want the family to believe my personal letter of apology was insincere and merely used to seek leniency from this court. My remorse and regret is a daily reminder to a life of goodness, a man of thirty years who knew no crime. That in a single moment of time was erased.

I was and still am the same man; a caring, loving husband and father, a law abiding member of society who sought only to be a good husband, father, and future medical doctor. Your honor, I would humbly ask, in the face of this horrible tragedy, this grief I have caused, that you would consider the good and positive aspects of me and the good and positive things that can be accomplished if given the opportunity.

I am reminded of a story of the great President Abraham Lincoln

*during the Civil War. A young man name Roswell McIntyre was draft-
ed. During a battle he became frightened and went A.W.O.L. Later,
he was apprehended and court martialed and sentenced to be shot for
desertion. Roswell's mother appealed desperately to President Lincoln saying 'he needed a second chance.' After much judicious thought, Lincoln
wrote a letter giving Roswell a second chance at life. In his letter, Lincoln
remarked, 'I have observed that it never does a boy much good to shoot
him,' That letter was taken from the body of Roswell McIntyre who died
in battle after having been given a second chance to redeem himself in some
way. President Lincoln showed great wisdom and courage in declaring
there is always time to try again. There is always some redemptive value
in a man's life.*

*I apologize to this court, its appointed officers, the citizens of the county,
and the state of Illinois. But most importantly, I apologize to the family."*

It seemed the judge was moved by what he read and called
for a two hour recess to ponder his sentence. I thought the
judge would retire to his chambers, fall on his knees and seek
God's face. I began to pray that God would move upon the
heart of the judge for compassion.

Recess over, I was shuffled back into the courtroom. The
case was called to order and the judge began to speak. "We
are back on the record. The State's Attorney is present along
with the defendant and his counsel. The court has considered
pursuant to the sentencing statutes and the evidence which
was received upon the jury trial of this case. The court has
also considered the pre-sentence investigation, as well as the
evidence, information, and testimony given by both parties in
aggravation and mitigation. The court has further considered
sentencing alternatives.

The sentencing statute requires the court to consider in im-
posing sentence the statutory factors in aggravation as well as
the statutory factors in mitigation. With respect to the statu-

tory factors in aggravation, the court finds that the sentence being imposed is necessary to deter others from committing the same crime.

With respect to the statutory factors in mitigation, the court finds that the defendant does not have any history of delinquency or criminal activity and has led a law abiding life prior to the commission of this crime. I have further listened to your family members. It is obvious they care about you and are concerned for you. However, that fact and the fact that you have never been in trouble are dwarfed by the facts of the crime you are convicted of.

You have been convicted of first degree murder and found guilty of the special verdicts of the aggravating factor of brutal, heinous, indicative of wanton cruelty.

I sentence you to a term of natural life in the Illinois Department of Corrections, without the possibility of parole. Good luck to you, sir!

Good luck! Good luck? I prayed under my breath, "God, kill him." I was put back in that fetid drunk tank under a suicide watch. Two hours later they let me back into the cellblock. Word had already made it back to the guys that I had been sentenced to natural life without parole.

In the ten months prior to trial and sentencing I had led many men to Christ. Despite my situation, circumstances, sentence, anger, and bitterness I thought it was important to show these men my faith in and trust in God. Sadly, many of the men I had led to Christ saw what happened to me and said, "If God would do that to you, I've got no chance." They essentially renounced their faith. This caused me such anger. It was such an opportunity to show God's great mercy, yet I felt the enemy got the victory, stealing the souls of the men I had worked so hard to win for the kingdom of heaven.

Great calamity came and the day of days was over. I was a convicted felon sentenced to natural life in prison. I was of no use to God now.

CHAPTER 2

During the next few weeks of waiting to be transferred, I became embittered. I felt like Naomi in the book of Ruth. In the story, Naomi was experiencing some very difficult times. Her husband had died and she was left with her two sons Mahlon and Chilion whose names meant "puny" and "pining." Then the two sons died. Naomi's circumstances were so dire that she wanted to change her name from Naomi which means "pleasant" to Mora which means "bitter."

"And she said unto them, call me not Naomi, call me Mora: for the Almighty hath dealt very bitterly with me. I went out full, and the Lord hath brought me home again empty: why then call ye me Naomi, seeing the Lord hath testified against me, and the Almighty hath afflicted me?"
- Ruth 1:20-21

I felt the same way, that God had testified against me and the Almighty had greatly afflicted me. I began referring to myself as Mora. Steven means "king" and I did not feel like a king. I was Mora – "bitter."

I wanted to see if God had any care for me at all so I devised a plan. Looking back now, it was ridiculous but in the end it served its purpose. I placed an empty shampoo bottle in the bars and said, 'God, if you are God and you still love me, remove that bottle from the bars." Now, we were not allowed to place anything in the bars and every day, several times a day, the guards would tell me to take it down. I was defiant. What could they do? I had a life sentence. Are you going to take away my birthday? Day after day that bottle remained in place, as stubborn and defiant as me. Each day that passed, I felt compelled to remove the bottle from the bars.

Finally, one day one of the guards threatened me with a trip to the "hole" if I didn't remove the bottle from the bars. With great sadness I began walking towards the bars to remove the bottle. I kept thinking, "This is it. God hasn't removed the bottle. It's proof that He does not care and has no love for me." As soon as I removed the bottle, my spirit spoke, "It's about time. I have been trying to get *you* to remove that bottle for five days."

I was both angry and elated. Angry because I had been expecting a holy ball of flame or something miraculous to move that bottle but elated because I now understood fully that God still cared about and loved me. You see, I was expecting a miracle, a sign while God was expecting my obedience and faith.

The next morning I was processed for transfer to the maximum security penitentiary at Menard (Chester), Illinois. This facility had housed notorious prisoners like members of the Charlie Berger gang, John Wayne Gacy, the infamous clown killer who killed many young boys and men. Also, calling Menard home at one time was Richard Speck who murdered eight nurses in the Chicago area, and Henry Brisbon the I-57 killer, also known as the most dangerous inmate in the Illinois Department of Corrections.

Taken to a holding cell, I was placed with six other convicted felons that were being transferred. All were eighteen to twenty-one years of age. Their sentences ranged from one to three years and with their county jail time all would be released from prison within 61 days.

When I entered the holding cell the nervous chatter stopped suddenly. These kids knew who I was and what I had been convicted of. Basically, they were hometown hoodlums who thought they were the "big man" in town. In reality, they were just scared kids that finally got caught with enough methamphetamine to get them charged and convicted of a felony.

All of us were manacled, shackled, handcuffed and belly-chained. We were then led down to an awaiting transport van. Because I was considered the highest threat level, I was placed in the back of the van while the other six guys sat on the bench seats in front of me.

It was a crisp November morning. The fresh air felt magnificent as I breathed in deep, cool waves of air. The sun was extraordinarily bright. This was the first sunlight I had seen in ten months. Our county facility was a sealed unit with no outdoor access or recreation. The rays of sun stung my eyes causing them to water involuntarily. The tears streamed down my mottled white cheeks leaving behind the remnants of their salty existence as I could not wipe them away.

With everyone loaded and secured, we began the one hour trip to Menard prison. I cannot say it enough, I was angry and bitter. Each step of the process only served as another irritant. During the transport, the young guys began laughing and joking about what they were going to do when they arrived in prison. They talked openly of getting tattoos, smoking, drinking some hooch or scoring some marijuana and getting high.

I became incensed at these fools and snapped, "You think you're going to a maximum security joint and take over? I'll make sure all the killers and rapists know that you punks think you're coming into their house to take over." There was no more laughing and joking. I was going to prison for life. They would be home in 61 days.

The transport guard looked back, laughed, and said, "Doc, that's pretty harsh but maybe these boys will get a good stiff dose of reality." Menard was the southern Illinois reception and classification center so I knew these kids would do two weeks there and then be shipped off to low medium security facilities. I just wanted to scare them a bit.

As we crested a hill and rounded a long curve, Menard penitentiary came into view. It was an ominous sight and the tension in the van became palpable. I yelled, "Not so funny anymore, is it?" It caught them off guard as I saw all six flinch. I laughed at their fear. On cue, the weather turned as we pulled in the parking lot. The crisp sunny day suddenly became dark, cloudy, and blustery cold. There was a storm coming.

After exiting the van we stood side by side. The youngest kid, only eighteen and smaller than me, nervously remarked, "Doc, you think they will let me cell with you?" He was the loudest and most vocal braggart of them all and it was time to teach this kid a lesson. I looked at him with my "crazy eyes," smiled and said calmly, "I'm gonna sell you. If I can't sell you, I'm gonna kill you." The poor kid burst into tears standing in the parking lot. The transport officer chastised me, laughed, and then whispered in my ear, "You might have just changed that young man's life." The officer knew me and knew what I was trying to do, scare him straight. That was the goal.

We were processed in and it turned out the young kid, Josh, and I were celled together. Upon learning of our cell assignment, I kept up the pressure, making statements like, "I wonder how many flushes it will take me to dispose of your body." When we finally made it to our cell, Josh took the top bunk and pulled his knees up to his chest. With a quiver in his voice he asked, "Doc, you're not gonna sell me or kill me, are ya?"

I began laughing so hard. This did little to allay his fears. He thought I was a maniac but I was only laughing at his fear and ignorance.

Reassuring him that I was not going to hurt him or sell him for food, we set about getting our bunks made up, cleaning the cell and generally getting everything, what little we had, in order.

We made a homemade deck of cards out of paper and crafted a set of six dice out of soap to play Yahtzee. We had no television, radio, or anything to read other than my Bible and our orientation manuals. It was going to be a long few weeks with nothing to do or read while awaiting classification and assignment.

Some time later there came shouts of, "On the new, come to the bars." That meant us. "On the new" meant new inmates. We stood at the bars awaiting the inmate worker who was working his way down the gallery pushing a plastic cart and handing out brown paper bags that were filled. The worker shoved two bags through the bars and we opened them up to find extra bars of state soap, a two-inch toothbrush, a small toothpaste, a bottle of shampoo, and a roll of toilet paper. The worker made his way down the gallery and soon returned.

"Hey! You THE Doc?" he asked. I was caught off guard as I did not know anyone in prison. Reluctantly, I acknowledged who I was and inquired how he knew me. He shoved an extra bag through the bars and said, "Lifers take care of lifers." This was my first indication of the tenuous camaraderie in a maximum security prison.

I asked if he would spare an extra bag for my cellmate and he obliged, remarking, "I like the way you think, not just looking out for yourself." I asked again how he knew me. He explained that they, other prisoners, had been watching my case on the news and waiting for me to arrive. That seemed unsettling, but he went on to explain it's just a way to look out for guys. It seemed a foreign concept to me that convicted felons would look out for a guy coming in on the new.

I was apprehensive, even unnerved but he reassured me it was men simply helping other men who had the misfortune of coming to Menard. How could hardcore convicted criminals show any sympathy, empathy, or kindness? Even more perplexing was, why? This did not fit the narrative I had learned growing up in Texas that all inmates were wild rabid animals incapable of feeling, asocial, and psychopathic. However, I would remain guarded until I learned the ways of prison life.

The worker stayed at our cell answering my many questions. He explained the daily routines, procedures, and schedules. My cellie and I had an advantage with the information we learned; information in prison is invaluable. Once he left, the new inmates in the neighboring cells began asking questions about the information we had gleaned. It was like feeding a ravenous litter of puppies. The questions were fired in rapid succession and the answers were slow and clear, at least to those questions that could be answered.

Three hours into a life sentence and I had already been blessed with favor. I did not see it then but as I write I see it was God's favor. I was just too angry with God to recognize it.

Night seemed to come interminably slow. It was eerily quiet on the gallery, a fact that I would later learn is not the norm. Prison is loud, offering a cacophony of relentless noise. Exhausted from the emotions of the day, I lay down to sleep a fitful sleep.

At some point in the night I felt a shove. Not a gentle nudge but a push. Thinking it was my cellie, I jumped out of the bunk ready to fight. He was lying on his side, facing the wall, snoring softly. I lie down and fell back asleep only to be awaken by a push and a voice that said, "Get up! Read Isaiah 53:8."

Now, this was a true move of God. I was mad now. I'm in prison for life and God is going to wake me up at whatever time it was to read scripture? I grabbed my Bible and began angrily slapping at pages until I turned to Isaiah 53:8. In the dim light I read, *"He was taken from prison and judgment ..."*

I lay back down and began complaining aloud to God. Why me? Why destroy my family? Why take me away from my children? Statistics show children without a father are more likely to get in trouble, have premarital sex, teen pregnancy, sexually transmitted diseases, more likely to be molested or raped. WHY MY CHILDREN?

God replied, "Are you a better father than I am?"

I deflected and replied, "God, you said I was going to be a doctor."

"No, I said you were going to be a HEALER. You are going to bring healing to many souls."

I rolled out of the bunk, my knees hitting hard on the concrete floor and began to weep, crying out for forgiveness. A scripture came to mind that I recited aloud.

"For I am persuaded that neither death, nor life, nor angels, nor principalities, nor powers, nor things present, nor things to come, nor height, nor depth, nor any creature, shall be able to separate me from the love of God which is in Jesus Christ my Lord." – Romans 8:38-39

I was comforted and assured, yet I still had anger. God, in all of His omniscience knew this and it would take a very long time for me to release it. I would serve God but there was always that ember of anger. Day one was over – "life" to go.

CHAPTER 3

S everal months later I was grinding through the mundane daily routine of prison life, still angry and bitter. Wake up, wash up, drink a cup of lukewarm instant coffee, watch the news, brush my teeth, go to chow at nine a.m., drink a cup of coffee, nap, watch TV, drink a cup of coffee, dinner at 3:30 p.m. The routine varied only when we had showers (twice a week) and recreation.

I isolated myself in a cocoon of bitterness, rationalizing that the other prisoners were grown men who had obviously been told about God, Jesus, salvation, etc. They surely did not need me to tell them. It felt as if I were alone.

I would pray, crying out to God for hours and my prayers seemed to bounce off the cold cement ceiling of my cell. There was no comfort. There was no joy. There was no peace. All I had was a little – a very little – faith and a lot of hope. I had no direction, no purpose until one day I read:

"Where there is no vision the people perish."- Proverbs 29:18

I was perishing ever so slowly. Essentially, I had the death penalty. I was just doing it on Illinois' installment plan. My sentence was not "life," but better described as "existence."

I began praying for vision, God's vision and purpose for my life. Two particular scriptures kept coming to mind but I ignored them. I was waiting on a booming voice, a true vision, a miracle. I wasted a lot of time due to my lack of knowledge of how God works. How does God work? Any way He chooses. In this instance, it was through quiet persistence in my spirit to read specific scriptures. A light bulb went on and I finally got it. A small lesson learned. Small but invaluable.

The first scripture was:

"Go ye therefore and teach all nations, baptizing them in the name of the Father, the Son, and of the Holy Ghost: Teaching them to observe all things whatsoever I have commanded you and lo, I am with you always, even unto the end of the earth." - Matthew 28:19-20

This is the bedrock scripture for all Christians, the "Great Commission." It seemed pretty straightforward but I was only reading the words on the page, not digesting the Word of God and understanding it. I began to pray and meditate on these two verses. Then came spiritual insight and I could see the two verses in a completely new light.

My spiritual eyes, ears, heart and mind were opened to this new commitment to and old commission. First, it was so pointed in its command "Go." You really cannot interpret that to mean anything other than its plain language. How do you go? Simple, you go by going, just as you would pray by praying, think by thinking, and love by loving. It is putting feet to your faith.

Take for example the call of Abram (Abraham).

"Now the Lord said unto Abram, GO forth from your country, and from your relatives and from your father's house to the land which I will show you."
— Genesis 12:1

Note Abraham's response.

"So Abraham went forth as the Lord had spoken to him."
— Genesis 12:4

Abraham went in obedience. God instructed him to go. He did not give him a plan, a path, even a direction. Just go. Leave everyone behind who you could rely on for help, trust God and "go forth." Today, the tendency when God tells us to "go" is we immediately begin praying: "Who? Me? Who is going to support me? What am I supposed to do? When do you want me to go? Where do you want me to go? How am I supposed to get there?"

Take the first step of faith like Peter did when he stepped out of the boat and began walking on the water. God will not do for you what He has commanded and given you the power to do. When God says, go, just go in faith.

Second, in the Great commission, note it is personal in its call. "Go, ye." Who is "ye?" Ye is YOU. Over the years, I've heard this verse misquoted more times than not. Why? Most people want to ignore and avoid the personal nature of the call. They will say, "Go therefore ..." but conveniently forget the "ye." Why? The "ye" is too personal and requires action. Most of the time it is an uncomfortable action, a sacrifice of sorts. Another reason someone will say, "Go therefore ..." is that they are endeavoring to shift the responsibility away from themselves and on to someone else.

Let's look at the book of Jonah, a familiar story to most. *"Now the word of the Lord came to Jonah the son of Amittai saying, 'Arise, go to Nineveh ...'"* – Jonah 1:1-2

Nineveh was a city, along with Babylon, that was established by Nimrod. Nineveh means "we shall rebel." It was a godless city that included idol worship and extreme cruelty to prisoners of Israel. Jonah did not want to go to Nineveh because he knew that if he preached the word of God as instructed, and the Ninevites repented, that God would spare their lives. Jonah was not willing to allow the enemies of Israel the opportunity to be spared. Of course, we know how that worked out for Jonah.

This is the same rebellious attitude many people today exhibit towards prisoners. They think if they preach the gospel to them or show them love then they may accept Christ. If prisoners accept Christ then they would have a Christian obligation to love them and care for their spiritual wellbeing.

You see, God chooses specific people for His specific purpose to go to specific places. In the case of Jonah with, "Here I am but you have called on the wrong guy. I'm booking a cruise to Tarshish," Jonah's response could not have been more different than the prophet Isaiah's response to his call:

"Then I heard the voice of the Lord saying, 'Whom shall I send and who will go for us?' Then I (Isaiah) said, 'Here am I. Send me."
- Isaiah 6:8

Many people are on their own personal yacht sailing towards their own proverbial Tarshish. Your Tarshish could be many different things. It could be your family, your job or your hobby. Whatever it is it represents rebellion. There are but two paths in life; obedience and the will of God, or disobedience and rebellion.

You can be assured that God has a certain and specific calling on your life that only you can do. Your life is full of value and potential waiting to be released and utilized. Each and every person is called to be an integral part in the body of Christ.

Earlier, I mentioned that the call of God is personal. Some people believe that the book of Jonah is an allegory and Jonah himself is an allegorical character. Jonah was a real, literal and historic man.

"The word of the Lord came to Jonah the son of Amittai." – Jonah
1:1

Moreover, why would Jesus make mention of Jonah in Matthew 12:39-41 if he was merely an allegorical character?

Just as Jonah's call was personal so is ours. Now we have the Holy Spirit that God uses to speak to our hearts. "From the heart the mouth speaks." Think about that. It is the very words that God speaks from His mouth that is deposited into a person's heart by the Holy Spirit.

Next, the call of the Lord has a purpose. In the context of the Great Commission the purpose was threefold: 1) to make disciples, 2) to teach, and 3) to baptize. God called Jonah to go to Nineveh to:

". . . preach against it, because its wickedness has come before me."
— Jonah 1:1-2

Jonah's purpose was to cry out against the wickedness of Nineveh. God's purpose was to call the people to repentance. Jonah had only one task to fulfill and that was obedience to cry out against the wickedness of Nineveh. He was not to be concerned with the outcome. That was God's responsibility.

When God calls you to a specific task you are simply to obey the call. Do not be concerned with the outcomes. When God called me to go into the prisons, it did not mean I was to pursue a medical degree, support a prison ministry, or become a medical missionary. I had a task to be a healer but I rationalized in my own mind what the outcome should be. I booked a ticket on Tarshish Cruise Lines and jumped aboard the ship "Get me the heck outta here!"

I was not willing to go to the prisons and cry out against their wickedness. I couldn't because of the many sins I harbored in my own life. I could not speak out against pride when I was a very prideful person. I could not speak out against ambition and success when my entire life was focused on being smarter and more successful than the next person. I could not speak out against pornography while I was viewing internet pornography. In hindsight, it was no wonder I fled to Tarshish. I was fleeing from my own rebellion and wickedness.

Jonah's choice to flee was not unexpected. It did not catch God unawares. The same is true for you and me. We weigh our options, make our choice and follow through with our plans to do wrong. However, there is no escaping the sight of God. There is no place you can run. There is no hiding place where you can escape the will of God.

"Can a man hide himself in hiding places so I do not see him? Do I not fill the heavens and the earth declares the Lord."
— Jeremiah 23:24

In this day and age it is common for people to flee from complicated and burdensome problems. It is easier to run than to face the difficulties head on. It is easier, faster, and cheaper to get an abortion than to raise a child. It is easier to get a divorce than to make the effort to save the marriage and family.

In past generations, abortion and divorce were relatively rare phenomena. Now, legal, moral, and ethical changes in ideology have changed the rare into the routine.

Jonah's downfall came as a result of his own plans. He thought he could take the easy way out when in reality he was:

". . . fleeing from the presence of the Lord." — Jonah 1:10

I only wish that I would have remembered the words of King David.

"Where can I go from your spirit? Or where can I flee from your presence? If I ascend to heaven you are there; if I make my bed in Sheol, behold you are there. If I take the wings of the dawn, if I dwell in the remotest part of the sea, even there your hand will lead me and your right hand will lay hold me."
— Psalms 139:7-10

I thought for a certainty that I could flee the presence of the Lord. By becoming a medical missionary, but my sin distorted my true calling.

Just as Jonah was unconcerned with the eternal souls of the people of Nineveh, I, too, showed no concern for the eternal souls of those men and women in prisons. I knew or thought I knew about the people in prison. They committed crimes, they were brutal and heinous, not only to the public but to each other. To me, they did not deserve a merciful God.

When I read the first two verses of the fourth chapter of Jonah, I came to realize why I ran from God's call.

"But it greatly displeased Jonah and he became angry. He prayed to the Lord and said, 'Please Lord, was this not what I said while I was still in my own country? Therefore, in order to forestall this I fled to Tarshish, for I knew you are a gracious and compassionate God, slow to anger and abundant in lovingkindness and one who relents concerning calamity.'"

– Jonah 4:1-2

I could not believe that God would give his grace, mercy and lovingkindness to convicts, felons who brutalized people or terrorized their communities. I did not want any part of that. I was angry and went looking for a ship to flee. It could have been the Titanic, the S.S. Minnow from Gilligan's Island, The Love Boat, a canoe, kayak, or paddle boat. All I knew was that I was not going to minister to prisoners. I was going to minister to people who deserved to hear the good news of grace, mercy, and lovingkindness. In other words, I rationalized that I could more effectively minister in my own Tarshish (medicine) instead of Nineveh (prisons).

I found a ship just like Jonah did. To find something necessarily implies that you are actively searching. I began college as a business major but loathed the mundane coursework. I wanted to do something exciting. Then came my call to prison ministry. Thanks, but no thanks. My ship was sailing for the

"Isle of Medicine."

Medicine was exciting, naturally easy for me to learn, and it felt right. Just because I had found a ship, it did not make it right. Everything seemed to be working out great but I was soon to learn my trip to Tarshish (medicine) when God called me to Nineveh (prison) would cause a storm of calamity in my life. I was going overboard.

Have you ever stopped to consider the costs of disobedience? Of course not. Once you choose the road of rebellion you begin paying a toll, a fare for your sin and disobedience. Disobedience has costs. Jonah paid his own fare (Jonah 1:3).

Running from God is the most expensive thing you will ever encounter. What did it cost me? It cost me my beautiful wife, family, my career, finances, reputation and, finally, my peace and joy.

Finally, the "Great Commission" is powerful in its companionship. "The Great Commission is based upon and backed by the authority of the risen and exalted Lord who promises to be ever present with His people." Note the word *commission* or better *co-mission*. You will not go alone. You will go with the assurance and authority of God and Father, His Son Jesus, and the Holy Spirit. You and I are co-partners with the Holy Trinity to not only "go" but to "do" and "complete" the mission we have been called to do.

"I will never leave you or forsake you so that you may say confidently that the Lord is my helper." – Hebrews 13:5-6

It is axiomatic that all born again Christians are called to fulfill the Great Commission of Matthew 28:19-20. It may include witnessing to your family, or someone in the grocery store, on campus, in a dorm, at a homeless shelter, in a prison. Wherever you are, wherever you go, anytime, anywhere, you are called to

"Go ye therefore and teach all nations, baptizing them in the name of the Father, the Son, and of the Holy Ghost: Teaching them to observe all things whatsoever I have commanded you and lo, I am with you always, even unto the end of the earth." - Matthew 28:19-20

The second scripture that God had so impressed upon my heart was:

". . . for many shall be called but few are chosen." – Matthew 20:16

I had read this verse many times before and viewed the words "called" and "chosen" as synonymous. However, there is a distinct difference. The "Great Commission" is a general call to all Christians to share the gospel and the love of Christ. Notice I used the word "share." To share means that there is a personal involvement, a personal sacrifice of your time and effort. A great illustration of this principle is found in the book of James.

"If a brother or sister be naked (poorly clothed), and destitute of daily food; and one of you say to them, depart in peace, by ye warmed and filled; notwithstanding ye give them not those things which are needful to them, what doth it profit? – James 2:15:16

Anyone can speak about love or talk about the Bible but what does it profit the person who needs to hear the gospel of salvation or feel and experience unconditional love?

Next, to be chosen is to be taken from among those who were called and selected for a specific task required by God. Moses is a perfect example. He was raised in Egypt under the tutelage of the best teachers, craftsmen and leaders. He was groomed for a position of leadership over people. However, Moses made a tragic mistake and murdered an Egyptian which was an act punishable by death. Moses fled and ended up on the backside of the desert keeping the flock of Jethro, his father-in-law. This prince of Egypt was now relegated to the position of a lowly shepherd.

After forty years Moses was prepared for the position and work God had chosen him for, to lead the children of Israel out of captivity.

"And the Lord said, 'I have surely seen the affliction of my people which are in Egypt, and have heard their cry by reason of their taskmasters; for I know their sorrows: And I am come down to deliver them out of the hand of the Egyptians, and to bring them up out of that land . . ."
– Exodus 3:7-8

"Come now therefore, and I will send THEE unto Pharaoh, that thou mayest bring forth my people the children of Israel out of Egypt."
– Exodus 3:10

Moses was chosen for this specific task of leading the children of Israel out of Egypt and their captivity. He had the dual pedigree to stand before Pharaoh and the children of Israel. His qualifications included being raised and educated in the house of Pharaoh. Moses was groomed to be a leader. Yet, he learned and possessed the humility and gentle nature of a shepherd. In God's eyes Moses was now uniquely qualified and selected for this great task.

Because God had asked Moses to participate in an uncomfortable action, Moses claimed to be flawed. He had a speech impediment. This reminded me of a story I once read.

Several years ago there was a display of crocks created by a potter who had made them well over one hundred years ago. The crocks had been discarded by the potter because they had become misshapen or flawed in the firing process. He placed the flawed crocks in a scrap pit behind his business. Over the years, his work became well known and highly collectible. When the damaged pottery was excavated from the pit, it was deemed valuable – not because it was beautiful but because of who made it.

This story is a reflection of God's children. We are all flawed in some way but our worth or value is not derived from how we look, talk, or dress. We are valuable because of who created us and that was God! Despite the fact that Moses was a murderer, a criminal and fugitive who had a speech impediment, he was chosen by God for the task of leading His people, His children out of captivity.

"Moses, His CHOSEN stood before Him . . ."
Psalm 106:23

No matter what your circumstances are right now, God wants to use you. You are valuable in God's eyes because you are His creation. God is **CALLING** you first to repentance and salvation. Then and only then will you be **CHOSEN** to perform your particular "God job."

Armed with this new revelation knowledge, not only did I know for certain that I was called as a Christian to fulfill the "Great Commission" by sharing the gospel of Christ, His great love, sacrifice and salvation but I was chosen by God as a healer of lost souls. I did not know the who, what, when and where but I did know the why – **OBEDIENCE**. I resolved to make my life's motto "Yes Lord."

CHAPTER 4

—◦◦⌒◦◦—

Whit is the first command to man in the Bible?
You shall have no other gods before me (Exodus 20:3)?

No, that was the first of the Ten Commandments. The first command was a command of OBEDIENCE.

"And the Lord God took man (Adam) and put him into the Garden of Eden to dress it and to keep it."

- Genesis 2:15

Adam was commanded to tend the garden. Obedience is the overarching umbrella to a right relationship with God. For us today we know that our relationship with God begins with faith in Jesus Christ as our Savior but it is obedience that evidences our right relationship with our Heavenly Father.

I like the analogy of the umbrella because if we stay under the umbrella of obedience in the midst of the storm, we will not be soaked by the perpetual rain of sin and persecution. If we remain under the umbrella of obedience, we will be protected from these things.

Notice I said "protected." That is because we are still subject to the storms of life and all that goes on around us in the natural world. Look at the sins listed in Galatians 5:19-21. They are exclusively dealing with the physical or fleshly world.

"Now the works of the flesh are manifest which are these; adultery, fornication, uncleanness, lasciviousness (lewd, lustful, salacious), idolatry, witchcraft, hatred, variance (to engage in an act contrary to an established rule), emulations, wrath, strife, seditions (rebellion), heresies, envying, murders, drunkenness, reveling ..." – Galatians 5:19-21

By comparison, the umbrella of obedience is made up of and supported by the fruit of the Spirit.

"But the fruit of the Spirit is love, joy, peace, longsuffering, gentleness, goodness, faith, meekness, and temperance."

- Galatians 5:22-23

Now, if you choose to step out from under the umbrella into disobedience, i.e., the sins listed in Galatians 5:19-21, then you are no longer protected but you subject yourself to the storms of the works of the flesh.

Have you ever seen two people caught in a downpour where one person has an umbrella and the other person does not? The one who has no umbrella, no protection from the storm makes a dash for their car. They may have a purse, newspaper, or briefcase to try to cover their head. When they get to their car they begin to wrestle and fumble to find their keys. All the while their flesh is getting pelted with the rains of the storm.

When you observe the person with the umbrella who is protected, they will stroll casually to their vehicle and with ease get out their keys and enter their vehicle. Outside the umbrella of obedience the storms of life rage while under the umbrella of obedience we can be assured that we are protected.

One of the greatest examples of obedience is Noah which can be found in Genesis 6-9. Here began the destruction of the earth.

"Then the Lord saw that the wickedness of man was great on the earth, and that every intent of the thoughts of his heart was only evil continually."

- Genesis 6:5

"Then God said to Noah, 'The end of all flesh came before me; for the earth is filled with violence because of them; and behold, I am about to destroy them with the earth. Make for yourself an ark of gopher wood...'"

Genesis 6:13-14

God goes on to give specific instructions and dimensions. In verse 22 we find

"Thus Noah did according to all God commanded him, so he did."

Genesis 6:22

You have to understand that up to this point it had never rained upon the earth. "Apparently, God suspended a vast body of water in vapor form over the earth, making a canopy that caused conditions on the earth to resemble those inside a greenhouse." Yet, God was asking Noah to build a boat! Can you imagine the ridicule Noah was subjected to? Think about how that conversation went with his wife. "Sweetie, uh, well uh, I found favor with God." When you find something that means you were actively seeking for it. So Noah had to have been actively seeking God's favor.

You know his wife rolled her eyes. Then Noah says, "Sweetie, well uh, God wants me to build us a boat to live in with a pair of all the animals of the earth." I can imagine she probably scoffed, "You? Noah? I can't get you to take the garbage out! I could never get you to change a diaper. Besides, what do you know about building a boat?" But that is exactly what Noah did.

According to Genesis 6:18 God chose Noah for this task and established a covenant relationship with him. "Covenant (Hebrew *berit*) occurs for the first time in Genesis 6:18. It signifies that the maker of the covenant obligates himself to keep the commitment as long as the favored recipient remains

OBEDIENT." Here, the Lord obligates Himself to preserve Noah throughout the coming destruction of the earth. Noah, in obedience, must build an ark and enter in to preserve life according to God's instructions.

Can God count on Noah? God authored the covenant but it could not be effected without Noah's obedience (see Genesis 7:1). If Noah does not build the ark and enter in, Noah and all life will perish, but so will God's plan and purpose to rule the earth through Adam and His promise to crush the serpent through the woman's seed (see Genesis 3:13-15), In other words, the future of salvation rests on Noah's obedience.

Can Noah count on God? To be sure, God calls upon Noah to trust Him to keep His threat to wipe out the earth and His promise to preserve him, his family, and all of the animals. If God does not send the flood, Noah would waste years of his life building the ark and would become a laughingstock of history. And if God does not keep His promise to preserve Noah and his family through the flood, their obedience would be in vain. However,

"Noah did according to all that God commanded him."
Genesis 6:22; 7:5

So you can be certain that if God has chosen you for a specific task, He has obligated Himself to see it from fruition to completion.

In my case, I refused to start a prison ministry in the Danville Correctional Center in the east-central Illinois town of Danville. Years later, my best friend and ministry partner sent me a newspaper article extolling the benefits and successes of the thriving prison ministry at the very facility I was chosen to "go unto." Just because I was rebellious and refused to do the will of God did not mean God's plans were thwarted. On the contrary, God found a willing, receptive, and loving heart to bring the gospel to the men I rejected.

Because of my disobedience, I stepped out from under the protection of the umbrella into the storm named Rebellion and Sin. Therefore, God's obligations of blessings upon my life were void until I took the first step of faith back into obedience and God's covenant.

"'Come now, and let us reason together,' said the Lord, 'though your sins be as scarlet, they shall be white as snow; though they be red like crimson, they shall be as wool. If you are willing and OBEDIENT, you shall eat the good of the land.'" - Isaiah 1:18-19

CHAPTER 5

I was incarcerated in a maximum security penitentiary. I did not know how to start a prison ministry. I did not know how to love the unlovable men. Nor did I want to befriend people with whom I had nothing in common. I didn't know anything about drugging, thugging, pimping or robbing.

Praying for hours, days and weeks, I begged God, "How do I start a prison ministry?" Finally, God replied, "Get out of the boat." What did He mean by 'get out of the boat?" I scanned the pages of my Bible's concordance for the word "boat" and found a familiar passage of scripture.

"But the boat was already a long distance from land, battered by the waves; for the wind was contrary. And in the fourth watch of the night He (Jesus) came to them walking on the sea. When the disciples saw Him walking on the sea, they were terrified, and said, 'It is a ghost!' And they cried out in fear. But immediately Jesus spoke to them saying, 'Take courage, it is I, do not be afraid.' Peter said unto Him, 'Lord, if it is you, command me to come to you on the water.' And He said, come, and Peter got out of the boat ..." – Matthew 14:24-29

At that moment I knew how to start a prison ministry. Just as Peter asked, "Command me to come," I asked, "How do I start your prison ministry?" and God answered very clearly. Have faith, get out of the boat, and take the first step. That's all God is looking for, an obedient first step of faith.

I began to search the scriptures in earnest for the call and commission of men. To my amazement, I began reading a story that so mirrored mine that I actually thought that this was the Holy Spirit causing me to read the words as if it were my own story. The story was the call and the commission of Ezekiel.

"Now, it came about in the <u>thirtieth</u> year, on the <u>fifth</u> day of the <u>fourth</u> month ..."

- Ezekiel 1:1

Now, this caught my attention. Why? Any prisoner can tell you without hesitation the exact date of his/her incarceration. Mine happened to be when I was thirty years old (the thirtieth year) in the month of April (the fourth month), on April 5th (the fifth day)!

Ezekiel 2:3 begins, "Then He said to me, 'Son of man ...'" I had to stop because as I read the phrase *Son of man* I could hear my name.

"Then He said to me, 'Son of man (Steve), I am sending you to a rebellious people who have rebelled against Me; they and their fathers have transgressed against me to this very day.'"

Ezekiel 2:3

At this time the children of Israel were captives of Babylon. In other words, they were **PRISONERS**!

"I am sending you to them who are stubborn and obstinate children, and you shall say to them 'thus says the Lord God.'"

— Ezekiel 2:4

If you are an inmate or a former inmate, you know how stubborn and obstinate prisoners can be. Most of the time their attitudes stem from rebellion, pride, greed, need for power, or anger.

"As for them, whether they listen or not — for they are a rebellious house

— they will know that a prophet has been among them. And you son of man (Steve), neither fear them nor fear their words though thistles and thorns are with you and you sit on scorpions; neither fear their words nor be dismayed at their presence, for they are a rebellious house. But you shall speak my words to them whether they listen or not, for they are rebellious. Now you son of man (Steve), listen to what I am speaking to you; do not be rebellious." — Ezekiel 2:5-8

As anyone who has ever been incarcerated can attest, you are truly living among the thorns, thistles, and scorpions in prison. Thorns and thistles are irritants and aggravators that cause a measured amount of pain and can be difficult to get rid of. The same is true in jail or prison. The noise is nonstop and cacophonous. There is never any silence. For some reason, toilets in prisons and jails sound like mini jet engines. I often wondered if they were designed to effect maximum decibel levels as an intentional irritant to inmates. In prisons and jails a flushing toilet at two a.m. can be heard the length of the gallery or the entire cellblock. It is also well known that the sting of a scorpion can be very painful. As well, the pain of acquaintances or prison "friends" who tell lies, slander, backbite, and rumor monger against you can be very painful.

It was clear that Ezekiel's ministry to a rebellious people would be very discouraging due to their rebellion, stubbornness and obstinance. So too would be my ministry. I had always believed that I was going to be a doctor, a medical missionary to Mali, West Africa. That would have presented many challenges, most notably the language barrier. I, along with my wife and children would have had to learn the language, customs, and courtesies of the Malian people.

But, the story of Ezekiel, my story, continued

"Then He said to me, 'Son of man (Steve), go to the house of Israel (prisoners) and speak my words to them, for you are not being sent to

a people of unintelligible speech or difficult language, whose words you cannot understand, but I have sent you to them who shall listen to you; yet the house of Israel (prisoners) will not be willing to listen to you since they are not willing to listen to Me. Surely they are stubborn and obstinate. Behold, I have made your face as hard as their faces. Do not be afraid of them or be dismayed before them.' Moreover, He said to me, 'Son of man (Steve) take into your heart all my words which I shall speak to you and listen closely. Go to the exiles (prisoners) and tell them whether or not they listen ...' I went away embittered in the rage of my spirit and the hand of the Lord was strong upon me. Then I came to the exiles (prisoners) who lived beside the river Chebar (Mississippi).
- Ezekiel 3:4-11, 14-15

The maximum security prison I was in was located literally across the road from the Mississippi River, more proof that Ezekiel's story was my story.

As I read this passage over and over again, much like Ezekiel, I became embittered. In Ezekiel's case he was embittered because of the obstinance of the people who would make his ministry that much more difficult. In my case, I was embittered with God. I could have been a great medical missionary and should have been a great doctor. I could have been a great husband and father, yet God was calling me to "bring His word" to the prisoners.

In my heart I protested. Why should I cast my pearls (gospel) before the swine (Matthew 7:6)? God, you know

"... a dog returns to its own vomit and a pig, after washing, returns to wallowing in the mire."
— II Peter 2:22

God finally reminded me:

"... do not be rebellious like the rebellious house."
— Ezekiel 2:8

As well as:

"...like emery I have made your forehead."
– Ezekiel 3:8

Emery is used for grinding and polishing. Truly, God had made me as one of the prisoners and I naturally adopted a hardened face. Already hard-headed, the question was would I be hard-headed (rebellious) against God or would I be hard-headed (obedient and steadfast) for God? If there was one thing that I had learned thus far, rebellion equals chastisement from God and chastisement is almost always painful in some way. You see, our obedience and faith cannot be manifest until we are chastised and corrected in our thoughts, beliefs and actions.

This principle was exemplified when Jesus, along with Peter, James and John were coming down from the mountain. There they saw the disciples and a crowd gathered. Jesus wanted to know what they were discussing. One person in the crowd replied:

"Teacher, I brought my son possessed with a spirit which makes him mute; and whenever it seizes him, it slams him to the ground and he foams at the mouth, and grinds his teeth and stiffens out. I told your disciples to cast it out, and they could not do it."
– Mark 9:16-18

In His frustration, Jesus replies:

"O unbelieving generation, how long shall I be with you?' Bring him to me. And he asked the father, 'How long has this been happening to him?' And he replied, 'From childhood it has often thrown him both in the fire and into the water to destroy him. BUT IF YOU CAN do anything, take pity on us and help us.'" – Mark 9:19, 21-22

Now, the next verse has been read in different ways and each provides its own context. The first is

"And Jesus said to him, 'If YOU can believe, all things are possible to him who believes.'" - Mark 9:23

Here, the emphasis is on the father to believe. However, another version reads

"[IF YOU CAN?] All things are possible to HIM who believes."

Personally, I believe the latter version is more correct. Why? We read in Mark 9:19 of Jesus' exasperation and in the latter interpretation it carries on the exasperated feeling in Jesus' speech. I believe that Jesus' response was one of righteous indignation. "What do you mean, IF I CAN? All things are possible to Him (the Son of God) who believes." Jesus knew that he possessed the faith to believe while the father's faith was not so. Therefore, his mindset had to be corrected so that his faith could be manifested.

"Immediately the boy's father cried out and said I do believe …"
- Mark 9:23

How does this apply to you? If God has chosen you, yet you have doubts and unbelief in your heart, the Word says

"…as a man thinks, so he is." – *Proverbs 23:7*

Therefore, you would be a doubter and an unbeliever in need of God's chastisement and correction that you may know that you have power that God has given you to fulfill His call upon your life.

Properly chastised, I began to submit to God's commission. However, I still could not believe that I was God's choice for a prison minister.

CHAPTER 6

Not knowing what to do next, I stepped out of the boat. I started by writing things down on paper. It started with a ministry name and a mission statement. The words came so quickly, so fluidly and so exact. The words manifested themselves in my head faster than I could write. "Lord, please slow down. I cannot write that fast." There was something welling up in me and it felt like I would burst if I did not get it on paper.

The seed of the ministry was planted. I once heard a famous evangelist say, "A seed is planted with a destiny inside of it. It has a destination. With every destination, there is necessarily a journey."

For the next several months I worked, went to the yard (recreation), prayed and read my Bible. During work hours and yard time, I pretty much made myself unavailable for friendship. In my short time of incarceration, I had already experienced several instances where my trust was betrayed. This, coupled with the fact that I was incarcerated because of the betrayal of my wife caused me to be deeply scarred emotionally, psychologically, and spiritually. I hardened my face, pursed my lips, and basically did not acknowledge the people who tried to interact with me.

I am a runner. I love to run so I ran a lot on my own, hour after hour, mile after mile. Sometimes guys would settle in beside or behind me while running and begin to chat me up. Didn't they get it? I just wanted to be left alone, completely alone.

Then one day while running it felt like I had been shot in the knee. I crumpled to the ground knowing instantly that I had suffered major ligament damage. I was taken to the prison healthcare unit and was diagnosed with a sprain and given ibuprofen. I disagreed vehemently, but was told even if it were torn ligaments they would not be repaired. As long as I could walk (limp) up and down stairs, ligament repair surgery was considered cosmetic. Besides, the healthcare unit provider, Wexford Health Services, a private for profit contractor had a "one good leg policy!"

Later that night I was once again angrily praying. On top of everything else I was now lame and letting God know about it. Then I heard in my spirit, "My grace is sufficient." Now I was enraged. "I don't want your grace. I want a healed or surgically repaired knee."

Again, "My grace is sufficient." I thought of the story to the Apostle Paul. Paul was given a thorn in the flesh. He implored God on three separate occasions to remove the thorn but God told Paul, "My grace is sufficient."

I knew at that time I was not going to be healed or get the surgery that I needed. God had a plan and it included a painful thorn.

I could no longer run, play basketball, handball or any other sport because of the instability in my knee. In essence, God was directing the situation in which I was forced to interact with other inmates. So I began to walk the perimeter of the yard.

One day I met a giant of a man, six foot five inches to my five feet five inches. He said, "Hey Doc." I replied, "Hi, Bill." We walked the entire two and a half hours of our yard period and never spoke another word. This pattern played out for months. Then one day Bill broke the silence. Understand, we never spoke. I knew nothing about him except that he was the leader or chief of his prison gang at one time.

Bill looked down at me with an expressionless face and in a monotone voice calmly said, "I killed my wife and tried to burn her body but couldn't get the fire hot enough. Buried her on my property." Now, what do you do or say to someone who is six feet five inches tall, roughly 280 pounds, was a gang chief, looks crazy and speaks in an emotionless monotone voice?

As we rounded the end of the yard where the phones were placed, I said, "Hey Bill, I've got to make a phone call. I'll catch up to you later." I broke out for an empty phone. Man, I was scared! I picked up a phone and pretended to talk to someone for over an hour.

Was this why I was lame? To walk around with psycho killers, gang bangers and the like? The answer is an emphatic YES! I did not like it one bit. Men seemed to be gravitating to me and began to treat me like a priest, sharing their personal stories, talking about their particular cases and confessing crimes they got away with.

At night, I would lie in my bunk and, as always, angrily pray. "God, how do you expect me to tell these men about love when no love is being shown to me? How am I supposed to tell them about restoration and reconciliation with their families and children when there is no restoration and reconciliation for me? How am I supposed to tell them about forgiveness when there is no forgiveness for me?" Then came the reply to my whining, complaining questions. "It is not about you. It is about my son Jesus."

During the following weeks I was trying to understand how being lame was going to help start a prison ministry. Until one day I was asked to come to a prayer group in the gym. I could not do any other physical activity so I agreed.

There I met an extraordinary man. His name is Allen Buckner. As soon as I saw him I knew instantly he would be my ministry partner. Allen could not have been more opposite of me. He is black, I am white. Races are not supposed to mix in prison. He was a former gang leader. I knew nothing about gangs or gang life. Allen was talkative and loud. I was more thoughtful, pensive and quiet. He would witness to a pole. He would tell anyone, everyone about Jesus. I would not. He was from the north while I was from the south.

We began spending a lot of time together in fellowship and prayer. Soon we became best friends. I approached Him to be a part of the prison ministry and without hesitation He agreed.

We had a plan and the beginning of a ministry team. Mending Broken Wings Prison Ministry was born. Although I was still angry and bitter, Allen loved me and prayed for me.

CHAPTER 7

The adjustment to incarcerated life was not an easy one. I was not transitioning to my new life very well. However, like Ezekiel, I would bring a form of the gospel to the men but did not really care if they accepted or rejected it.

"Steve (son of man) I have appointed you a watchman to the house of Israel (prisoners). Whenever you hear a word from my mouth warn them from me. When I say to the wicked, you shall surely die; and you do not warn them or speak out to warn the wicked from his wicked way that he may live, that wicked man shall die in his iniquity, but his blood will I require at you hand. Yet, if you have warned the wicked and he does not turn from his wickedness or his wicked way, he shall die in his iniquity; but you have delivered yourself."
– Ezekiel 3:17-19

I had no problem with this message. Choose it or lose it.

But something started to happen, a subtle change. Allen was a God-sent blessing. He embodied what it meant to be a true Christian and friend. We would pray together, talk, listen, and support each other. I never had a true friend so this was new to me. Allen was showing me that it was okay to love these men. He loved me despite my crime and conviction. He loved me in spite of my "whiteness." Racism is rampant in prison and we were both subject to physical violence for violating the "stay with your own race" code.

For example, one day while walking the yard together, Allen split off to talk with some other men. I continued walking and soon an unknown caucasian man approached and said menacingly, "You're going to stop messing with the niggers or you're going to get your head split open."

I was stunned. I continued walking when a black man approached and said, "You're gonna stop talking with the brothers or we're gonna split your head wide open."

By this time I was confused, nervous, and hypervigilant anticipating an attack. I went to a black man I worked with and told him the story of what had just transpired. He disappeared for a few minutes. I continued walking, figuring I could check to see if anyone was following me. Several minutes later a group of four men, two white and two black, were walking towards me. This was it. I began bracing up, muscles tensing and adrenalin flowing. I was not taking a beat down without getting in a few good licks myself.

They approached and said, "Hey Little Doc. We put the word out. Ain't nobody gonna touch you. All you do is try to help people no matter who or what they are." These four men I had never met invited me to walk with them. They basically set up a security perimeter around me. I later learned that all four were members in their respective mobs. This was to show anyone who thought they were going to do me harm that they would better think twice. It was an unorthodox act of kindness when races were supposed to take care of their own.

I remember reading a quote once, and I am paraphrasing, "How dare you have the audacity to question God's creation because of their skin color. God created man in His own image."

This incident along with the addition of Allen in my life caused me to want to know more about godly friendship so I began to pray. Who is a true friend? It is someone who accepts you as you are now. A true friend is someone who will laugh and cry with you. A godly friend will be a prayer partner, an intercessor, even a shield to deflect criticisms. A godly friend will be honest and trustworthy.

So what does the Bible have to say about friendship? It gives clear direction on the types of people we are to avoid. The first are slanderers and gossips.

"He who goes about as a slanderer reveals secrets. Therefore do not associate with a gossip." – Proverbs 20:19

A true friend will not reveal the intimate secrets you reveal. However, a gossip is one who wants to be known as the person with final knowledge and who controls and disseminates that knowledge. God said do not even associate with someone like this.

"He who covers a transgression seeks love, but he who repeats a matter separates intimate friends." – Proverbs 17:9

A godly friend may graciously overlook a transgression but if he or she holds it over your head or repeats the transgression to take advantage, this is someone who will cause friendship to be broken and is to be avoided.

A second type of person that should be avoided as a friend is a person of anger.

"Keeping away from strife is an honor for a man." – Proverbs 20:3
"Do not associate with a man given to anger; or go with a hot tempered man, or you will learn his ways and find a snare for yourself."
– Proverbs 22:24-25

Hot tempered people can fly off the handle easily and most of the time they seek to induce fear in others. This can be a learned behavior that is dangerous both physically and spiritually. That is why God counsels us to avoid these people.

*"A man of great anger shall bear the penalty. For if you rescue him,
you will only have to do it again."*
— Proverbs 19:19

"It is futile to rescue a man given to anger, for his temper will repeatedly land him in fresh trouble."

Another caution espoused regarding friendship is:

*"A man of too many friends comes to ruin but there is a friend who
sticks closer than a brother." — Proverbs 18:24*

This is a caution that by choosing friends indiscriminately you may bring yourself trouble. It is also a warning that you do not have to befriend the popular or cool person. These people have too many friends. We all possess the innate desire to want to be liked, to fit in. We just need to be prayerful about the friends we allow in our lives. They can have a significant spiritual impact, whether positive or negative. They will impact your life in some way.

The second part of Proverbs 18:24 advises that a genuine friend will stick with you through thick and thin. This was what I was finding in my friend Allen. He was so genuine. He would correct my transgressions lovingly.

For example, one day while walking to the chow hall a correctional officer who was known to be particularly rude was, well, being himself. I made it obvious that I was looking for his nametag.

He asked gruffly, "What are you looking for?"

"Just looking for your name," I replied.

He barked, "What for? You gonna file paperwork on me?"

I said, "No, I'm going to pray for you." He seemed to soften a little and then I added, "I'm going to pray God kills you," and I walked away.

On the way back from the chow hall that officer was trying

to be very congenial with me. It seems I put the fear of God in a man who did not believe in God. I knew it was the wrong way and it was done in a wrong attitude. My friend Allen counseled and corrected me.

Another time I was praying like I did every night. I was lying on my back. At eleven o'clock p.m., five nights a week, one particular officer would come down the gallery for a count check. Every night, I lay there with my eyes closed, holy hands lifted to God, and my lips were moving. Three things were immediately obvious. First, I was present and accounted for. Second, I was alive. Not many dead inmates hold their hands in the air while their lips are moving. Third, I was praying.

This officer took great pleasure in shining his flashlight directly on my eyes and shaking it back and forth until I moved position. The next night he did this but I did not move but rather spoke out loud, "God, if it be Your will, strike him blind." That officer never again flashed his light in my eyes. Again, my friend Allen lovingly chastised, counseled, and corrected me.

Some years later I was speaking with that officer and he let me know that he was an atheist. If you do not know, an atheist means someone who does not believe in God. "A" equals absent, while theist is a belief in God. Thus, we get the term atheist, or someone who has an absence of belief in God.

I explained that there was no such thing as a true atheist. He disagreed and began expounding on how there could be no God. I told him if there was no such thing as God then why did he work so diligently to disprove the existence of a non-existent Being. His very efforts to disprove that God does not exist acknowledges that there is in fact a God.

Next, I explained that he could not be an atheist because he actually believes in God. I referenced that night on the gallery and asked, "Why have you never shined your flashlight in my eyes again?"

"You were praying for God to strike me blind!" he remarked emphatically.

"But if you do not believe there is a God then you have nothing to fear, right?

He pondered a few minutes and then wanted to know more about my God. I was glad to share and witness to him about Jesus and the gospel of salvation. That man made a decision to accept Christ. My job was done. However, it might have never come about had it not been for the loving chastisement, counseling, and correction given by my godly friend Allen. Years earlier, I had come to despise that officer. I had a wrong mindset, attitude, and heart. It had to be corrected and Allen was one edge of God's two-edged sword. Because of Allen, I was able to witness to and lead an enemy to Christ. I planted, someone else watered, but God truly got the increase.

This same principle was being worked in my own heart. Allen had sown a seed of friendship. It was being watered by other godly men, and God was sure to get the increase.

One night, while praying deeply, fervently for my friend Allen, I quoted

"Greater love has no man than he lays down his life for his friend."
— John 15:13

Without thought and before I could stop the words from being spoken, the words, "Father, if it means Allen being released from prison, I will take his life sentence," flew from my lips. I was startled. Hold it, I said as I tried to take back the words. Not only could I not speak to retract them, my mind simply went blank and I could not even "think" the words to be retracted.

What was this? The word friendship pierced my heart. I began to weep. A piece of my hardened heart had been chipped away and exposed was a small portion of a soft, fleshy, receptive heart that allowed friendship to penetrate it. Allen was a true godly, genuine friend and he would make a great ministry partner. God had a plan.

CHAPTER 8

So many things in prison are unconscionable, mean-spirited and cruel. Though I was not a baby Christian, I was prone to vacillate in my faith when confronted with these things. One particular incident set me back.

A friend of mine had been diagnosed with terminal cancer and given only a few months to live. This man had been convicted of a drug crime and sentenced to twenty years at one hundred percent of the time to be served. His diagnosis came six months short of his release.

He immediately applied for a "compassionate discharge" so that he may spend his final few months of life with his family. He was not a violent offender, he had a drug case. Further, he never had a single disciplinary write-up. He was the model inmate who rehabilitated himself.

However, the state of Illinois did not see it that way. His request for a compassionate discharge was summarily denied. The staff callously remarked, "We want every day of your sentence. We own you until that time or until you die."

Two months later I received special permission to visit him in the healthcare unit. He was terribly emaciated, unkempt, and suffering. Prison healthcare is undeniably the worst form of "care." You are considered a nuisance, a drain on staff's time as well as their budget. My friend died the next day and I let the poison of bitterness seep into my heart.

On another occasion I met an older man named Mike. We became fast friends and he arranged a job for me working with him. Mike was 60 years old when I met him. He had been raised by the state his entire life. His mother had dropped him and his brother off at a catholic orphanage when they were still toddlers.

At the age of thirteen he was sent to a boys' reformatory. At eighteen, he was released and soon was in trouble. He was sentenced to "life." At that time it was "life" with parole after fourteen years and six months. He was out of custody for seven years when he committed another crime that netted him a total of 180 years serving at least fifty percent of his time before being released. Essentially, it was a life sentence.

Hearing his story, I was intrigued so I asked jokingly, "When did you know that you were destined to be a criminal?" Without hesitation he replied, "When I got into a fistfight with a nun!" I laughed heartily at the joke but as it turns out it was no joke.

At age 13, in the Catholic orphanage they sat down for lunch. He explained, "I began eating before the blessing was offered over the meal." The sister promptly began twisting his ear painfully so he turned around and punched her. This is why he was sent to the boys' reformatory.

Some years later, Mike began having mini-strokes. He did not want to suffer in prison so he attempted suicide. After his hospitalization we met up again and I wanted to make sure to share the gospel of salvation with him He accepted Christ as his personal Lord and Savior.

A few years later Mike was hospitalized with dementia and other health issues. One day I was asked by the cell house sergeant if I would be willing to be an inmate assisted living attendant for Mike. This meant I would live with him 24 hours a day, seven days a week and would care for him. I would change him when he soiled himself, bathe him, shave him and turn him every two hours. Basically, I would do the tasks that the regular nursing staff did not want to do.

To me, this would be an honor. I spent my adult life in selfish arrogance trying to be successful. However, this was an opportunity for me to be significant.

In prison nothing gets done quickly. I had to wait for the approval process to be completed. During this time, Satan began attacking me with selfish thoughts. "You are not going to have contact with the general population. You are not going to have anyone to talk to. You are going to be limited in your movement, confined to the healthcare unit."

In prison being able to move around meant being able to network with others to get things you wanted or needed. I fought off these selfish thoughts and resolved to forsake it all to help another man as he was dying.

Two weeks had passed and I still had not received the approval I needed. Then one day I received the message that Mike had died. I was once again angry because the last two weeks of his life were spent in agony and alone. I questioned God! I questioned my faith.

Now, sometimes I talk to God as if He were sitting across from me. I would make a cup of hot – better, lukewarm – cup of instant prison coffee and sit down and have a candid conversation with God. I call it "Java with Jehovah" time. This situation with Mike troubled me and I wanted to know why God would ask me to do something and then not follow through with it.

The story of Abraham and Isaac kept coming to mind. I

could not understand how Abraham being asked to sacrifice his own son related to me. Then I realized as Abraham was tested, so was I. Abraham's test was one of faith in God while mine was one of relinquishing faith in myself.

As I stated before, I was a very selfish individual. I had plenty of opportunity and motive to bail on a task that others would not do. I could have forsaken my friend for self or I could forsake self. I chose the latter.

Though my friend passed away, the final two weeks of his life were used to prove me, to teach me. This gave me a new appreciation for the scripture

". . . for the one who is least among all of you, this is the one who is great." – Luke 9:48

Earlier in the text we read that the disciples had been arguing amongst themselves.

"An argument started among them as to which of them might be the greatest. But Jesus knowing what they were thinking in their hearts took a child by His side, and said to them, whoever receives this child in my name receives Me. Whoever receives Me receives Him who sent me; for the one who is least among all of you, this is the one who is great." – Luke 9:46-48

The disciples were selfishly arguing who was going to be the greatest in the kingdom of heaven. Not for a moment did they think about the fact that Almighty God or righteous Jesus would be there with them. What a selfish thought to think that they would be greater than the King in His own kingdom.

You see, God does not desire that we be great. He desires us to be humble.

"But to this one I will look, to him who is humble and contrite of spirit."
– Isaiah 66:2

People are only as great as they think they are. But God can take the humble person and use him/her in whatever capacity they allow God to do so, and God will allow others to see that humble person as great.

This realization, or better yet, this revelation was a pivotal step in my spiritual growth and God's plan. The first step in God's plan was exposing and correcting my selfish attitude.

CHAPTER 9

Prisons and jails are cruel and mean. The atmosphere is tense, tempestuous, and wicked. The so-called "inmate ethical code" is a perversion like no other. It is pretty much adhered to by inmates and staff alike. Murder is okay but murder of a child is not. Any crime against a child puts you on the low rung of the inmate hierarchy. These inmates are rarely given the opportunity to hold a job as they are loathed. The same is true for anyone convicted of a sex crime. It is okay to murder an entire family as long as you did not rape a woman or molest a child.

Then there are the unwritten but accepted rules like which phones are for a particular gang. Another rule was not breaking or crossing lines during movement. This is when a gang moves together in a line. If you cross their line in front of them or cut in between, breaking their line, it was a sign of disrespect and you did it at your own peril.

Finally, everyone knows the rule no snitching! Being labeled a snitch could bring about physical reprisal. If you saw something and wanted to tell the staff what really happened, you are a snitch. Wanting to do the right thing is no excuse. Talking to internal affairs staff was taboo.

Violating any of the rules and any rules set forth by your

own gang subjected you to punishment. Punishment could range from not being allowed out of your cell, a "violation" which is a beatdown, or a "hit" being put on you.

This was so foreign to me. I could not understand how God could allow evil like this to exist. How could God justify using an institution so wicked and vile itself to punish people. These were but a few questions I was struggling with when I came across the book of Habakkuk.

You may be asking yourself, what and where is the book of Habakkuk? It is a very small book in the Bible, only three chapters in length, located between Nahum and Zephaniah. Suffice it to say, Habakkuk is not a well studied book by Christians, but it should be.

Not a lot is known of this minor prophet but his name means "embracer" because of his love for God. The book of Habakkuk presents a man with the same burning questions I had. Why did God permit wicked practices to continue unabated and how could holy God justify using the evil Chaldean (Department of Corrections) to punish others.

In this scenario, God had given Habakkuk a vision of the impending captivity of Judah. The Chaldeans were a particularly brutal people who took pleasure in the sadistic treatment of the Jews. Habakkuk cried out:

"How long, O Lord, will I call for help and you will not hear me? I cry out to you, 'Violence!' yet you do not save. Why do you make me to see iniquity, and cause me to look on wickedness? Yes, destruction and violence are before me; strife exists and contentions arise. Therefore the law is ignored and justice is never upheld. For the wicked surround the righteous; therefore justice comes out perverted." – Habakkuk 1:2-4

Wow! That sounds like a perfect description of prison or jail. Violence, contentions, strife. Christians are outnumbered ten to one, wicked surely surrounds the righteous.

Now, the strife and contentions mentioned in verse 3 were within the tribe of Judah itself and not with any other enemy so what were the great sins Habakkuk was referring to?

"Now it will come to pass when you tell these people all these words that they will say to you, 'For what reason has the Lord declared all this great calamity against us? And what is our iniquity, or what is our sin which we have committed against the Lord our God?' Then you are to say to them, it is because your forefathers have forsaken me, and followed other gods and served them and bowed down to them; but Me they have forsaken and have not kept my law. You too have done evil, even more than your forefathers. Behold, you are each one walking according to the stubbornness of his own evil heart without listening to me." – Jeremiah 15:10-12

The charge against Judah included forsaking God, idol worship, stubbornness and evil. This is what caused Habakkuk to ask the questions of Habakkuk 1:2-4. He could not understand how God would allow wicked practices to continue. The simple answer is that God does allow it to continue but be assured that God will call to account those who pervert His ways.

"Justice and judgment are the habitation of thy throne." – Isaiah 89:4

As I was studying the passages in Habakkuk and Jeremiah, I began to realize that I was like Judah. I had forsaken God's statues, precepts, and commands by allowing evil to rule my life through all manner of sin. I worshipped the idol of medicine. I was an adulterer. Medicine was my mistress. These are the sins that caused my internal strife and contention, that struggle between repenting and turning back to God or living a life of sin and disobedience.

In the answer to Habakkuk, God replied:

"Look! Observe! Be astonished! Wonder! Because I am doing something in your days you would not believe if you were told." – Habakkuk 1:5

God was going to cause the Chaldeans to take Judah captive as punishment for their continual sins. This was also the answer to my question of Why? I had to be taken captive by coming to prison. My sin had to be judged by righteous God and His justice must be served.

"My judgment is just. " – John 5:30

"Does God pervert justice? Or does the Almighty pervert what is right?" – Job 8:3

I was worried on numerous occasions, yet refused the warnings, reproofs and rebukes.

"He that being often reproved hardens his neck (becomes stubborn) shall suddenly be broken beyond remedy." – Proverbs 29:1

Broken beyond remedy does not mean destroyed or beyond repair. It means that in your brokenness, your circumstances cannot be remedied or repaired in your own strength and will. It is solely the grace and mercy of God to provide the remedy and restoration. No amount of human effort is going to change that. There is but one exception. You must submit yourself unto the Lord. You must repent or turn from your sin and evil ways. Finally, you must be obedient in keeping and walking in the way of the Lord.

Thinking you can will your way out of the situation of testify your way out of it will not work. Neither your money and influence nor your education and intellect help. There is but one avenue of remedy and that is submission, repentance, and obedience.

The next question Habbakuk asks is, "Why God will You use wicked people to punish Judah?" Remember, the Chaldeans were arrogant people who exhibited cruelty and violence toward the Jews. Habakkuk was perplexed.

"Your eyes are too pure to approve evil, and you cannot look on wickedness with favor. Why do you look with favor on those who deal treacherously? Why are you silent when the wicked swallow up those more

righteous than they?" — Habakkuk 1:13

Would righteous God allow unrighteous people who perform unrighteous acts to punish others? The answer is yes.

"You, O Lord, have appointed the (Chaldeans) to judge; And you, O Rock, have established them to correct." — Habakkuk 1:12

Doesn't this sound like our Justice system?

It is God's sovereign right as the Creator of heaven and earth and all that is therein to use any means or methods He wants to utilize. He is Elohim, the Creator. The God over all the universe and all life. The One who preserves you. And because He wants to preserve you, He can and will use any method necessary to see that you are corrected.

A perfect example of this is found in the book of Numbers chapter 22. Balaam was a "diviner." Some men of the tribe of Moab came to Balaam and asked if he would come with them and curse the Israelites. God told Balaam not to go and not to curse the Israelites.

Balaam was a lover of money and had a considerable reputation for his successful prophecies and was paid well. He wanted to go with the Moabites to collect the handsome fee. He thought he might convince God to change his mind and permit him to go.

God did grant him permission to go but expressed His anger because of Balaam's love of money (verse 22).

"Forsaking the right way they have gone astray, having followed the ways of Balaam, who loved the wages of unrighteousness."
— II Peter 2:15

Balaam saddled his trusty and faithful donkey and went with the leaders of Moab. Along the way an angel of the Lord stood in the way. When the donkey saw the angel of the Lord standing in the way with a sword drawn, the donkey took off into the field. Balaam struck the donkey to get it back on the path.

The donkey saw the angel of the Lord again. In an attempt to get away from the sword, the donkey veered into a wall and crushed Balaam's foot. Again Balaam struck the animal.

Finally, the donkey lay down because she saw the angel of the Lord with the sword. The donkey had enough sense not to proceed toward certain death. Incredibly, Balaam struck the donkey a third time.

Then the Lord caused the donkey to speak, asking, "What have I done but to save your life, for you to strike me these three times?" Balaam answered and the donkey replied. There was a running dialogue with this man and his donkey. Finally, Balaam's eyes were opened and he could see the angel of the Lord with the sword in his hand.

So, you can see, it is God's providence to use anything He wants to perfect His will. What was most incredible 1) that the donkey spoke, 2) that the donkey spoke perfect Aramaic or Hebrew, or 3) that Balaam carried on the conversation?

It is undeniable that God would use the evil Chaldeans as an instrument of punishment of His children of Judah. And God will use the judicial system as an instrument of punishment, reproof, and rebuke. He will use your captivity that you may live and not die, both physically and spiritually.

In the case of Judah, God would use the evil Chaldeans.

"Why have you made men like the fish of the sea . . . The Chaldeans bring all of them up with a hook, drag them away with their nets, and gather them together in their fishing net." – Habakkuk 1:14-15

Jeremiah had sounded the warning before.

"Behold, I am going to send many fishermen declares the Lord and they will fish for them." – Jeremiah 16:16

You have probably seen it on television or in the movies, how they call the new inmates "fish." I thought about this for some time and wondered why they call them "fish." Drawing from my own experience as a novice fisherman, the only answer I could come up with was the way the fish looked when you hook it or catch it in the net and bring it to the surface.

Effectively you have removed it from its natural environment. You have exposed it to conditions it is not suited for. The fish's eyes are bulging and look glassy. It is as if they are

"astonished in wonder" – Habakkuk 1:5

How could they be fooled? Next, you see the fish struggling to breathe, its gills pumping rapidly for the life saving oxygen it can only get in its natural environment.

This is a representative picture of those inmates who come in new. I have lived through my own fish phase. I have seen it on others' faces. I pitied them.

When I first arrived at Menard Correctional Center in southern Illinois and was waiting to be processed with six other individuals. I took notice of their faces. It was at this time I came up with my theory of the term "fish."

Their faces were blank. Their eyes were wide open and glossed over as if they were staring into darkness. Yet, you could almost see the question rattling around in their brain, how did I get caught up in this? They seemed astonished and in wonder at their captivity. And when that heavy steel door crashes closed and you are locked in a 5'x9'cell, it takes your breath away.

The first thing you do is try to take a deep breath of air but what you inhale is the acrid, fetid smell of incarceration. You look around and all you see is gray: gray concrete floors, gray concrete ceilings and walls and gray bars. You come to the realization that you are, in fact, a fish caught in a great, gray, steely mesh net called prison.

Habakkuk described the Chaldeans (the captors) as one who

"Enlarges his appetite like Sheol, and he is like death, never satisfied. He also gathers to himself all nations and collects to himself all people." – Habakkuk 2:5

Again, this is the perfect description of any prison system. Lawmakers and powerful unions have learned that corrections is big business. They make more laws, increase the penalties, build more prisons, hire more staff who pay more taxes, and purchase more products and services in their local communities.

The appetite for corrections has enlarged and is never satisfied. It does not matter who you are, where you are from, your religion, sexual orientation, education or socioeconomic status. Corrections will gather and incarcerate them all.

Finally, Habakkuk described the coming invasion and captivity by the Chaldeans.

"Though the fig tree will not blossom and there be no fruit on the vines, though the yield of the olive shall fail and the fields produce no food, though the flock should be cut off from the fold, and there will be no cattle in the stalls." – Habakkuk 3:17

What Habakkuk was saying is that the tribe of Judah would be stripped of everything.

This is also the scenario upon a person's incarceration. You are stripped of everything and solely dependent upon God. You are stripped of your freedom because you are incarcerated. You are stripped of your dignity as you are subject to humiliation, ridicule and strip searches. You are stripped of your pride, your clothes, individuality, choices of food, bathing, and even sleeping.

When we are stripped of all these things we become vulnerable and it is in this state of stripped down vulnerability that God can begin His correction, His sovereign work in our lives.

It is in these times when we are stripped of everything externally such as family, friends, spouse, jobs and money. When God wants to infuse his spirit in us, when the external is stripped away, then we can begin to surrender to God and focus on the internal, spiritual person God desires us to become.

Incarceration is not the end of your life. It can be the beginning of your new spiritual being and life if you can discover God's grace, mercy, faithfulness and love in the midst of this time of trial.

CHAPTER 10

———◦◦◦———

Throughout the Bible you can find many examples of people finding and recognizing the faithfulness of God in the midst of their tribulation. Is it possible for someone to experience the pain of incarceration and find God to be loving and faithful? Is it possible, through the trials and tribulations of incarceration, for the character of God to be revealed in and through us despite the crimes we were convicted of? The resounding answer is yes!

Though incarceration may be harsh and difficult, it has a purpose. That purpose is to bring you to God or bring you back to God. You can spend your time in anger and bitterness, continuing to live a life of sin or you can accept God's invitation.

"So He brought their days to an end in futility and their years in sudden terror." – Psalms 78:33

Your time of incarceration can be spent in futility and trouble or it can be productive and proactive, reaping blessings.

"For I know the plans that I have for you, declares the Lord, plans for welfare and not calamity to give you a future and a hope."
– Jeremiah 29:11

Instead of focusing on the negative, asking God, why is this happening to me? We should ask, how can God's glory be revealed to me and through me? In this question you can learn about the character of God in adversity.

One thing that you must understand is that nothing surprises God concerning our lives.

"Consider it all joy when you encounter various trials." – James 1:2

Notice it says "when" not "if." The trials, tribulations, pains, hurts, and sufferings will come but be assured that God is in control of all things and nothing happens outside of His will. When the various trials enter our life, they enter only by the permission of God. There are two compelling examples of this truth, Job and Peter.

In the book of Job we find that Satan wanted to try Job and sought the permission of God. God gave Satan permission but with the limitation that he could not touch Job himself. This was to be a specific attack against Job to expose his true motives for serving God. Job was wealthy, blessed of the Lord with family, finances, livestock, etc. However, Satan charged him with being selfish, serving God only because he had many things.

The next attack was to be against Job's body. Once again, Satan approached God for permission to try him and once again God gave His sovereign permission. However, He set the limits of the physical attack on Job's body that Satan could not kill him.

The second example is found in the book of Luke. The setting is the Lord's Supper on the Thursday before Christ's death.

"And the Lord said, 'Simon, Simon behold Satan has sought permission (of God) to sift you like wheat. But I have prayed for you that your faith may not fail; and you; when once you have turned again (to your faith), strengthen your brothers.'" – Luke 22:31-32

Here again, Satan needed the permission of God and it was

granted with limitation. The limitations are not expressly noted. However, when Jesus said, "but I have prayed for you that your faith may not fail," that necessarily implies that Peter's faith would be tested but would not be destroyed and he would return and strengthen those around him.

It is precisely these types of limitation that the Apostle Paul wrote about.

"God is faithful, who will not allow you to be tempted (tested) beyond what you are able." – I Corinthians 10:13

Read the story of Joseph found in Genesis chapter 38. Joseph had a dream that he would one day rule over his brothers and parents. This angered his brothers and they cast him into a pit. Eventually, they sold him into slavery.

Further reading reveals that Joseph was unjustly accused of trying to rape his master's wife. He was thrown into prison. Joseph did nothing to deserve this treatment but God had a plan for Joseph's life that included some major trials and tribulations but there were limitations. Joseph's dream did eventually come to pass as did God's plan.

So, when we read

"I know my plans for you and they are good and not evil."
– Jeremiah 29:11

You can be assured that God will see it through to completion. Though you may not enjoy the sufferings, like Paul, God admonishes:

"My grace is sufficient for you, my strength is made perfect in weakness." – II Corinthians 12:9

Be encouraged that whatever the nature of your trials, tribulations or sufferings, it is only by God's permission because He has a purpose and plan for your life.

When faced with difficulties we tend to spend an excessive amount of time and energy trying to figure out through our own logic the who, what, where, when how and why. After playing what I call "thought-chess" you may deduce an explanation and a plan to get out of the situation. I was guilty of this.

I am a very analytical person. I tend to think in terms of A-B-C, 1-2-3, black or white, if this-then-that. There have been times in my life when I would spend hours and days dissecting a problem. I could compile pages of notes, scenarios, conjecture.

In the end, I would develop a masterful outline, flowchart or "spiritual" roadmap. There was nothing spiritual about it because it was done in my own power. Looking back now, it seems so comical that I, the great cracker of the God code, could ever begin to discern the plans and purposes God had for me.

When you remain fixated on the who, what, where, when why and how, you are missing out on God's blessings. You should be asking, "What is God's purpose in this trial?" There will always be an earthly purpose and an eternal purpose.

Let's look again at Jonah. God commissioned Jonah to go to Nineveh, saying:

"Arise, go to Nineveh the great city and cry against it, for their wickedness has come up before me." – Jonah 1:2

The earthly purpose was to cry against the city to effectuate repentance so that an entire city would be spared. Imagine an entire population experiencing the mercy and grace of God. The eternal purpose was twofold. First, those who accepted the message could inherit eternal life. Second, and most important, God would receive glory.

You may ask like I used to, "Lord, how long will this last?" It will last until you wholly submit in obedience to God and His plan and purpose is fulfilled. You must remember, God is not moved by time. He is moved by purpose. You are probably saying to yourself, "That was God working in past biblical times." The Bible is clear:

"God is the same yesterday, today, and forever." – Hebrews 13:8

God has not changed. He remains faithful. His mercy and love endures forever. So, let me give you a personal example.

During my incarceration, I was sought out for a clerk position. The position entailed working with sensitive personal information of the staff. I had not applied for or even asked for the job. The supervisor sought me and offered me the job. After spending time in prayer, I was assured that this was the position I was to be in.

While on this job I had the opportunity to work with many different staff members, earning a good testimony with them. I worked in this job for over ten years which is extraordinary and unheard of in prison.

During this time I did not understand God's purpose for allowing me to be in this particular position. Now, after many years, I have come to understand. The job was a one-man job assignment so I worked virtually alone. It also came with a single—man cell but it was behind a solid steel door.

Many guys would not want to live alone behind a solid steel door. I, on the other hand, enjoyed the solitude and silence which is priceless in prison. This time allowed me to pray, praise, worship and meditate uninhibited. It allowed my faith to grow exponentially.

When on the job, I started to notice that staff began coming to me for advice or help with various problems they were facing. One man had a serious medical issue and brought his x-rays in for me to view.

Another officer came to me with a grotesquely swollen hand and explained he had already had x-rays done and they were negative. After a few questions about the circumstances leading to the swelling, I knew immediately what the problem was as I had previously seen a similar case.

I explained that he had a long slender thorn that was perfectly situated on top of a bone in his hand. The x-ray could not distinguish it from the bone. He went back to the doctor and, sure enough, another x-ray view revealed the foreign object. Immediate surgery was performed and the man's hand was saved.

Another time, a female staff member came to me for legal advice. I had been studying law, working on my appeal. She had been charged with her second DUI. She was facing mandatory jail time, fines, dismissal from her job and the loss of her children. I did some research for her and she received probation and a small fine, but kept her job and children.

The point is that God has a purpose for you where you are now. However, you have to know that when that purpose is complete, God will move you into another purpose. God is not static.

I had been on the job for over ten years and had garnered great respect and favor. Everything changed when a new supervisor began working in the office we shared. He did not like me from the first day he started and was offended that he would have to share an office with an inmate. It did not matter that I was the one doing his work which made him look good. Nothing I did could please him.

I began praying diligently for God to remove this man from his position. I rationalized that it was obtained through nepotism and favors from the new warden, his drinking buddy.

The man became belligerent, harassing and threatening. At one point I let him know that I was not here for writing bad checks. I clung to the job supposing I was to endure with grace but knowing in my heart it was time for me to move on.

God knew I was comfortable and would not leave the job on my own so He had to provide an irritant to get me to act. I liken it to trying to continue to walk when there is the smallest of pebbles in your shoe. It is an irritant that must be dealt with. It is a call to action. After you remove the pebble, you walk along comfortable with a sense of relief.

The job I had paid fifteen dollars a month. I had been praying for prosperity to be able to tithe more, give more offerings and to help others in financial need. God was trying to bless me with a better job with a better salary. I was trying to figure out how I was going to stay on my job but receive more pay.

Once again, I received an unsolicited job offer in the correctional industries program where my salary increased tenfold to $150 per month. I was prison rich! I experienced a direct answer to my prayer for prosperity but I would not have received the blessing without the irritant to move me out of my complacency and comfort into a new purpose.

You may feel that God cannot use you but I want you to know that God can use you. He will use you and He stands waiting to use you. A life submitted to God can reconcile families, create friendships, heal diseases as well as terrible wounds in the hearts of people we hurt or who hurt us.

It all begins with humbling ourselves before God and seeking His purpose. You cannot bargain your way out of God's perfect purpose. You can live in the freedom, love, and power promised by God through His Son Jesus. You can stop asking why, when and how and begin asking what? Lord, what is Your purpose? God will work in and through you. You will become an example of God taking

"what the devil meant for evil and turning it around for the good of those who love Him and are called according to His PURPOSE." –
Romans 8:28

CHAPTER 11

The only way to discover your purpose is to be in right standing with God. If you are reading this book, you may be in the midst of some terrible trial or situation. You may be incarcerated, have lost a loved one, are faced with a devastating diagnosis, or your spouse may have walked away from the marriage. Whatever situation you are in, you can turn it around if you will get back into right standing with God. How do you do that?

First, you come just as you are and exactly where you are right now. The scripture tells us:

"If anyone serves Me, let him follow Me: and where I am, there my servant will be also." – John 12:26

Since God is omnipresent, He is everywhere and everywhere includes where you are. You see, God is not afraid of the uncomfortable situation. He will meet you in prison, in the "hole" in the prison. God will meet you in the hospital, at the funeral, in the AIDS hospice, in the abortion clinic, or even in the divorce lawyer's office. Yes, God loves lawyers also. He is not afraid. It does not matter where you are or what your circumstances are, God wants you to come to Him. When we come to God, it pleases Him.

Of course, the best example of this is found in Luke 15, the story of the prodigal son. As the story goes, a man had two sons. The younger son asked his father for his share of the inheritance. The father relented and soon the younger son was spending the inheritance on the sinful pleasures of the world. Within no time at all, the young man was broke and had to take a job feeding the swine. His circumstances were so dire that he began eating the food, the slop that was for the pigs.

Finally, one day he came to his senses and said, "I'll go home and beg my father to hire me as a servant." When the young man made it home, his father saw him and began to run to greet him. The son confessed his sin with humility and purposed to again come into right standing with his father. The father accepted him back, not as a servant but as the son that he was.

Seeking God is not difficult. Many people believe their sin, status or situation precludes them from coming to God. However, God promises that if you will

"Call upon Me and come and pray to Me. I will listen to you. You will seek Me and find Me when you search for Me with all your heart. I will be found of you."
– Jeremiah 29:12-14

Take notice that it said "... search for me with all your heart." This means earnestly searching for God with the right attitude, with the expectation of finding Him.

In Luke 18, we find the story of the Pharisee and the tax collector.

"The Pharisee stood and was praying to HIMSELF: 'God, I thank you that I am not like other people, swindlers, unjust, adulterers, or even like this tax collector. I fast twice a week; I pay tithes of all I get.'" –
Luke 18:12

Pharisees were a very arrogant group. They felt as if they were more righteous than everyone else because they kept the traditions of the church. To be a Pharisee meant that one loved his position or status and loved to be seen and revered by others as righteous. But, notice three things that prove that he came with a wrong attitude.

First, he was praying to HIMSELF! In other words, he was elevating himself to a god equal with *the* God. Next, he began pointing out and condemning the sins of others. Would God condemn one of His own? I think not. However, this self-professed god readily condemned others. Finally, the Pharisee said, "I pay tithes of all I GET." He could not even acknowledge that God is Jehovah-Jireh, Provider. It is God who gives and we receive. However, this Pharisee is saying, "I get what is mine," instead thanking God for His provision and blessings. Of course, God could not act on such a prayer as the Pharisee's. He came with the wrong heart and haughty attitude. He did not come "searching for God with his whole heart." He came to boast of and proclaim himself.

By contrast:

"The tax collector, standing some distance away was unwilling to lift up his eyes to heaven but was beating his breast, saying, 'God be merciful to me a sinner.'"

– Luke 18:13

This man came in humility. So, the first step to searching for and finding God is to come to Him with a humble attitude.

Next, you must come with repentance or contrition which simply means being sorry for your sins.

"But to this one I will look to him who is humble and contrite of spirit."

– Isaiah 66:2

In the previous story, the Pharisee revealed himself to be self-righteous and showed no contrition though he knew the scripture which provides

"There is none righteous, no not one."
— Romans 3:10

Yet, he refused to acknowledge his own sin and unrighteousness. In short, he was arrogant and unrepentant.

Meanwhile, the tax collector was so ashamed of his sin that he refused to even look towards heaven and cried out, "... God be merciful to me, a sinner." This man understood his very sin nature and saw the need to confess his sin, to repent. You will not find or receive God's blessings without repentance. Your perceived personal goodness or rightness will not move God.

Third, you must forgive! Holding on to a spirit of unforgiveness is holding onto a spirit of offense and will prevent you from finding God. You should always be vigilant to perform a spiritual check-up on yourself and make certain you are not harboring unforgiveness in your heart.

You may be thinking, "Yeah, but my spouse cheated on me. My spouse walked out. My co-defendant snitched on me. God, why is this happening to me? I do not deserve this." This list is not all inclusive and these things may be true. Any example you may give may very well be true, too. I caused the death of my wife's lover and for many years I harbored unforgiveness of her as well as the deceased man. Can you imagine having unforgiveness for a deceased person? Ridiculous, right?

You may say, "You do not understand. I want revenge and I want justice. Am I supposed to forgive someone who is not sorry?" Seeking revenge is a flesh response and our flesh desires it. However, when you forgive that is a faith response and you put aside thoughts of revenge.

We are commanded to forgive not to seek revenge.

"Whenever you stand praying, forgive, if you have anything against anyone so that your Father in heaven will also forgive your transgressions.

But if you do not forgive, neither will your Father in heaven forgive your transgressions."
— Mark 11:25-26

By contrast:

"Never take your own revenge, beloved but leave room for the wrath of God, for it is written, 'Vengeance is mine, I will repay' says the Lord."
— Romans 10:19

The scriptures teach that we must be willing to forgive. We will be forgiven to the same degree that we forgive. If we are unwilling to forgive those people who have hurt us or done some type of injustice to us, we are the ones who ultimately suffer.

A final and no less important aspect to forgiveness is to forgive yourself. Refusing to forgive yourself is self-sabotage. Holding on to a wrong or perceived wrong that you have committed and refusing to forgive yourself is sin.

I could not forgive myself for causing another man's death. I condemned myself daily. I would not forgive myself, thinking that if I suffered enough through my self-loathing for my deadly action, this would give God cause to lessen His punishment. I refused to acknowledge my own birthday or celebrate Thanksgiving or Christmas.

In the facility I was in, they served a traditional holiday meal for both Thanksgiving and Christmas, complete with turkey and dressing and all the trimmings. It is the two best meals all year long and very few men miss them. As far as prison chow goes, this is the equivalent of five-star dining. For the first fifteen years of my incarceration, I refused to walk to the chow hall and eat these two meals reckoning that if the deceased man's family could not celebrate the holidays with their loved one, then I could not celebrate and enjoy the feast, either. In essence, I was acting as if I were dead.

While in the U.S. Air Force stationed at Clark Air Base in the Republic of the Philippines, I learned of a tradition the locals performed on Easter. It was called the "flagellation." The men would walk a certain route to their own crucifixion, like Christ. They did this as penance, atonement for their sins. Yes, they would eventually be nailed to a wooden cross. However, their crucifixion was not unto death.

During the march they would carry their crosses and whip themselves with a homemade "cat-of-nine-tails," a short whip-like apparatus that had bits of rock, metal or glass woven into the leather strands. Their backs would be bruised and bloodied just like Christ. The difference was these men chose to punish THEMSELVES.

Much like this tradition of flagellation, I chose to punish myself day after day, year after year. I became sullen, melancholy and clinically depressed. My relationships with family and friends suffered, my faith suffered and eventually I experienced a series of minor heart attacks.

Then one day a scripture came to mind so I grabbed my Bible and turned to read.

"There is therefore now no condemnation for those who are in Christ Jesus."
— Romans 8:1

Wow! What an epiphany. I am in Christ Jesus therefore there is no condemnation. If God is not condemning me neither should I condemn myself. I had to forgive myself.

The Bible tells us that He (God) casts our sins in the sea of forgetfulness. Yet, every day I chose to get in my rowboat of self pity and went fishing for "condemnation." To no surprise, it was readily plentiful to be caught. Now, with this revelation I could finally:

". . . lay aside every encumbrance and the sin (of unforgiveness) which so easily entangles us . . ." — Hebrews 12:1-2

CHAPTER 12

Earlier I mentioned contrition and repentance is in relation to God answering our prayers. There are many men and women who are incarcerated worldwide. If you have ever watched any docu-dramas such as "The First 48" or "To Catch a Predator," one of the most often repeated lines is, "I am sorry. I just want to go home." Oh, if it were just that easy. There is a significant difference between apologizing to save your own skin and apologizing in a sincere repentant way. There are only four things that move God: sin, repentance, prayer, and praise.

Sin has brought you to your place of incarceration. You broke the law, whether you broke man's laws and it has resulted in physical incarceration, or you broke God's law by your own choices and actions and it has resulted in spiritual incarceration. In either case, your sin is a cause for God to move and move He will.

In the book of II Kings, chapter 17, the prophet Jeremiah laid out the sins of the children of Israel that caused them to go into captivity.

First, they built watchtowers and fortified cities (II Kings 17:9). These acts showed their lack of faith in God's sovereign protection of their well-being. God had established a covenant with Israel. Therefore, it was His sovereign duty to protect them. Yet, Israel trusted only in themselves.

"If we are faithless, He remains faithful for He cannot deny Himself."
– II Timothy 2:13

This is a tremendous statement of the very character of God. He did not destroy the nation of Israel because they were faithless. However, he did allow for their captivity and in captivity he protected them.

So, the question is: What walls have you built around your life that prevent you from fully trusting God? In my own life, I had erected a great barrier against close personal relationships, as well as watchtowers of "perfection." I had to be perfect or at least guard the perception that I was.

I had developed serious abandonment issues as a child. My father walked out on our family when I was five years of age. This had a profound effect on me. Not only did he abandon us (me), he made no effort to be part of my life. Visits were few and far between, forced and strained. My father did not want my siblings and me to visit. When we did there was no warmth and no love. We were a nuisance only to be tolerated.

Next, on several occasions my mother dropped us kids off at a friend's house. We would later learn that she left instructions to turn us over to the Texas Department of Children and Family Services. Eventually, she would return several hours later, almost always intoxicated, high, or both. Imagine how much fear and anxiety this caused us small children who believed they would be torn from a parent, separated from siblings, and placed into strange homes.

On one occasion, at the age of nine I walked home from school (about a mile). I was known as a latchkey kid, always carrying the key to our apartment on a string around my neck. Upon arriving home, I found a note that informed me that my mother had left for the weekend, my sister was staying at a friend's house for the weekend, and my younger brother was sent to a babysitter. Attached to the note was a five dollar bill.

We were poor and I knew there was no food in the apartment, so to eat I was going to have to go the grocery store. Most nine year old boys who have been given five dollars would spend it on candy, soda or video games. I had to make a decision to be careful how I spent the precious little money entrusted to me, a nine year old.

I planned my menu before heading off to the grocery store. I settled on a pound of ground beef, a box of Hamburger Helper, a can of creamed corn and a loaf of bread. It totaled about $3.75. Remember, this was 1978. On the way home, I stopped at a fruit stand and purchased a few fresh plums.

The rationale for the menu went like this. Hamburger Helper was easy enough to cook and there would be leftovers so I could make it stretch over the weekend. I did not like creamed corn so I figured it would take me at least two days to choke it down. Next, a loaf of bread was cheap and bread was filling. I could make toast for breakfast and slather it with the government butter that we received each month. Besides, just about every family in our government subsidized housing complex received government cheese and butter. I figured I could borrow some cheese or butter to make sandwiches. To this day, I still believe that the best grilled cheese sandwiches are made with government cheese and butter.

The fresh plums were the real prize. Sure, I could have purchased some canned fruit but I had and still have a love for fresh fruits and vegetables.

Living alone for three days was a terrifying proposition for a nine year old boy. I survived but not without some lasting effects.

Finally, I had never had a birthday party. No pictures exist of me having a first or second birthday or any other year, either. My birthday is December 22ⁿᵈ, three days before Christmas. I got to pick one gift from under out Christmas tree but that meant I would receive one less gift on Christmas morning. I always wondered why my siblings, stepbrother and stepsisters included, got to have a birthday celebrations while I was always an afterthought.

Now, many years later, I get to celebrate my birthday with the most precious friend I have ever known. On or about my birthday each year my friend Donna travels about four hours one way to visit and celebrate my birthday in the prison visiting room.

These birthday visits are the highlight of my year, sharing a vending machine birthday meal and vending machine birthday pastry. However, they are much more than just another visit or a vending machine meal (which is incredible compared to prison food). My friend's birthday visits are affirmations from God that the child within wants to be loved and recognized. Donna's birthday visits are more than just blessings, they are affirmations that I am loved.

The next sin Israel committed was building sacred pillars (II Kings 17:10) when they had been instructed to tear them down.

"But rather you should . . . smash their sacred pillars . . ."
Exodus 34:13

Pillars are support columns that hold or prop something up. They are structural. If pillars are torn down the structure necessarily cannot stand.

Take for example Samson. Samson was a Nazarite. This meant he was bound by a vow of consecration of service to God. However, Samson met Delilah, a daughter of the Philistines and they were eventually married. Samson, a man of God, yoked or attached himself to an unbeliever. The Bible is very clear that a believer should not marry an unbeliever.

"Be ye not unequally yoked together with an unbeliever: for what fellowship hath righteousness and unrighteousness and what communion hath light with darkness?

II Corinthians 6:14

In the case of Samson, his pride and arrogance were his "pillars" all wrapped up in one thing, his hair. Delilah coaxed from him the secret of his great strength and then acted upon it. She cut his hair which was a breach of the Nazarite vow. He became weak and was quickly overtaken and taken into captivity. She not only weakened his physical strength but also his understanding and character. In captivity his eyes were put out. Samson followed after the lust of his eyes; therefore, the Philistines gouged them out. In short, Samson was forced into humiliating slavery.

Then one day the lords of the Philistine people came together to offer a sacrifice to their god Dagon for delivering Samson into captivity. They wanted to put Samson on display and mock the once great man of God. They ordered him to be brought to the feast of the sacrifice.

Next, they chained him in between two pillars. Samson put his hands on the two pillars and prayed for God to strengthen him one more time.

"And Samson took hold of the two pillars upon which the house stood, and on which it was borne up . . . "– Judges 16:29

Samson received the supernatural strength that he prayed for and "tore down the pillars" so that all the Philistine people who came to worship a false god perished. It is believed that three thousand people perished.

So, the question is this: "What pillars do you have erected

in your life that support your life of sin? Pillars can be many and varied. For example, drugs, sex, and money can be pillars.

I had four pillars in my life: pride, arrogance, a hyper-driven work ethic and medicine. Just like Samson, these pillars had to be torn down. How were they torn down? Like Samson, I was taken into captivity (incarcerated) and my pillars were torn down by the Holy Spirit and the Word of God.

What pillars is God asking you to tear down? You can be certain that you can tear them down or God will tear them down. Are you ready and willing to ask God what pillars he wants to remove from your life? Are you ready to tear down the supports and rest securely on the firm foundation of God?

"Nevertheless the foundation of God stands sure, having this seal, the Lord knows them that are His. And let everyone that names the name of Christ depart from iniquity." – II Timothy 2:19

The next sin committed by Israel that led to their captivity was setting up Asharim (an idol) and serving those idols.

"They set for themselves sacred pillars and Asherim . . . They served idols concerning which the Lord had said to them, 'You shall not do this thing.'"
– II Kings 17:10,12

Notice that pillars and idol worship are closely associated. Pillars supported the altar for the sacrifices to these false gods. Tearing down the pillars is the first step. When you tear down the pillars, you necessarily tear down the altar where the idols are worshipped. However, there is still the issue of the idol.

Asherim were idols carved of wood that represented the Canaanite goddess Asherah who is thought to be the mother of seventy gods. The people would place the Asherim on the high hills overlooking their fields, groves and orchards. They believed so much in the power of the Asherim that one would be placed as the base of every green tree. Asherah was worshipped as a fertility god or god of fruitfulness.

An idol is an object that is adored and worshipped. It can also be defined as excessive admiration and devotion. Now that we have a working definition: What idols(s) are you worshipping? Is it your television, smart phone, the internet? Ouch! That question hurt, right? Did I get a little too personal? How much time do you spend watching television or on your phone or surfing the web? What idols do you excessively adore that are preventing you from serving the one, true, living God?

Now, take half of that time and think about how your life can change if you used it to read the Word of God, pray, praise, or meditate. Wow! You could see great changes in your marriage, with your children, and interpersonal relationships. Most of all, you will reap the benefits of a close personal relationship with your heavenly Father.

Did I have idols? To be sure. These idols had to be removed from my life. Incarceration accomplished this and brought me to the place where I would seek God rather than spend mind-numbing hours in front of the television or on the web. Once again, the choice is yours. You can remove the idols or God will remove them through His sovereign circumstances.

Following on the heels of these sins, the children of Israel became rebellious.

"However, they did not listen but stiffened their necks." – II Kings 17:14

There are many synonyms for rebellion. These include defy, disobey, insubordinate, and obstinate. In other words, Israel became defiant, disobeyed God and became difficult to manage. Their rebellion had to be subdued.

"A rebellious man seeks only evil, so a cruel messenger will be sent against him!" – Proverbs 17:11

The cruel messenger sent against Israel was the wicked As-syrian nation who took them captive. The cruel messenger sent against me was the justice system and I was taken captive and incarcerated.

I can remember one specific incident that caused me great hurt and pain. It was at the point when I slipped into deep rebellion. After returning back to Texas from the Philippines, my wife and I began attending the church I had attended as a teen. I had lived with the pastor and his family before joining the Air Force so it felt like home and family. Soon after joining the church I was asked to be an usher. Over time, this led to the position of head usher and eventually, I was voted by the membership to become a trustee. A trustee's responsibility included overseeing the church's finances.

Upon discharge from the Air Force I had a job waiting for me. However, on the day I was to begin working, the news came that there was no longer a job available. I had separated from the financial security of the Air Force and now I had a three week old son and a new mortgage. There was zero income.

In my position as a trustee, I would review the financial requests and needs of church members as well as families in the community who needed financial help. The church would pay their bills or provide food from the food pantry.

One family had a daughter who had married and she in turn had a daughter who was born with severe medical issues. The family rarely attended church , only attending on Christmas and Easter. The church was willing to pay their mortgage and utilities. I had no issue with this.

During this time, finding a job seemed impossible. Things were becoming desperate financially. No matter how hard I prayed I could only find part time temporary work at minimum wage. It was humiliating to not be able to support my young wife and newborn son. Once again, those abandonment issues surfaced as I began to feel like God was abandoning my family and me.

Finally, I spoke to the pastor, the man who took me into his home when I was homeless, to seek financial help. Without help, we were going to lose our home. A "love" offering was taken up that totaled $246, not even half of our mortgage payment.

Next, I spoke to the head trustee about getting some groceries from the food pantry. He did not think it was good idea. My wife and I had given our time, money, efforts, and prayers to the church and people we loved. The investment paid off with, "Sorry, we cannot help." This angered me terribly and the abandonment issue hit me hard. Now my own church and friends were rejecting me.

How could the church take care of non-member families and fail to support one of its own member families and staff members? I immediately resigned my position. We had to sell our home and moved to Illinois to live with my wife's parents. This was particularly humiliating and served to highlight my pillar of pride that I discussed earlier. This one singular experience was the seed of my rebellion.

In short, I became as the stiff-necked, rebellious children of Israel. Just as it caused them to go into eventual captivity, it would also send me into captivity. It did not have to be that way for Israel. It did not have to be that way for me, and it certainly does not have to be that way for you.

The next sin Israel committed was rejecting the statutes and commands of God.

"They rejected His statutes and His covenant . . . they forsook all the commandments of the Lord their God." – II Kings 17:15-16

You may claim ignorance of God's statutes and commands.

The common saying in the legal system "ignorance of the law is no excuse" also applies to obedience to God's law. Surely, you have heard a sermon or have a mother, grandmother, aunt or other family member who has taken you to church. Regardless, God gave each of us a conscience to know the difference between right and wrong.

I know the commandments of God, yet I chose to forsake them. The first command that I forsook was attending church.

"Forsake not the assembling of yourselves together." –Hebrews 10:25

This act of rebellion prevented fellowship with other believers who could encourage as well as pray for me. It prevented me from hearing the teachings offered in sermons.

"Faith comes by hearing, and hearing by the Word of God. –Romans 10:17

Next, I gave up reading my Bible. Reading the Bible is akin to feeding your spirit. Just as you take in food to nourish your body, you read the Word of God to nourish your spirit.

"Man does not live on bread alone, but on every word that proceeds out of the mouth of God." –Matthew 4:4

Jesus is the bread of life.

"I am the bread of life; he who comes to me will not hunger" –John 6:35

Most people know the "model prayer" by heart.

"Our Father who art in heaven. Hallowed be Thy name. Thy will be done on earth as it is in heaven. Give us this day our daily bread . . ." –Matthew 6:9-14

This not only encompasses physical bread provided by God, it includes spiritual nourishment and spiritual growth. Do you eat only every few days? No, you eat to satiate your hunger to stay strong every day. Then why would you neglect your spirit for days, weeks, months or years at a time by failing to partake of God's Word?

In North Korea there is a severe ongoing famine. The food is strictly rationed. This famine is closing in on its second generation of the North Korean people. The average North Korean man is only five feet four inches tall, while his South Korean counterpart is five feet eight inches tall. The only difference between the two groups of people is the amount of food eaten.

South Korea is a free market, democratic nation that prospers and food is plentiful. The health of its people is significantly better only because of nutrition. The lack of food and nutrition has stunted the growth and contributed to the poor quality of health and life to the North Korean people. This principle applies to our spiritual life as well. I chose to forsake the reading of my Bible. Therefore, I chose to cut off my source of spiritual nutrition. My faith and spiritual growth was stunted.

Next, I forsook prayer. Prayer is fellowship with God. It is supposed to be an intimate interpersonal relationship. In a relationship it is necessary for both parties to communicate. Without reciprocal dialogue the relationship suffers. Prayer is not simply asking God for things. He wants to have a deep abiding relationship with you. I chose to end my prayer, my relationship with God. However, God did not forsake me.

Earlier I mentioned building walls. Here I built a great dam that choked off my spiritual lifeline. The Bible tells of those who accept Jesus as their Savior as being grafted in the vine. This means that we receive the benefits of nourishment, growth and fruitfulness (blessings) of the plant (Jesus).

But what happens if you cut off the source of water, sunlight or nutrients? The plant withers and eventually dies. This is exactly what I chose to do and my spiritual life began to wither. What statutes and commands are you forsaking that is causing your spirit to be dry, arid, and stunted?

". . . and they followed vanity and became vain, and followed after the nation which surrounded them." – II Kings 17:15

Vanity is something that is useless or worthless. In other words, Israel began chasing after the material things of life that are useless and worthless in the kingdom of heaven. Does this sound like you? It not only sounded like me, it was me! I chose to forsake the command:

"Do not love the world nor the things in the world." – I John 2:15

There is a consequence.

"Friendship with the world is hostility toward God. Therefore, whoever wishes himself to be a friend of the world makes himself an enemy of God."

James 4:4

I do not know about you but I have read the back of the book! If you have not read the book of Revelation, let me clue you in. God wins. The enemy is defeated and is cast into the prison of hell.

Is hell like a prison? The answer can be found in Revelation.

"I am He that lives, and was dead; and behold I am alive forevermore and have the keys of hell and death." – Revelation 1:18

Let's be clear. I am not saying that every person who commits the same sins as Israel will be condemned for all eternity in the prison of hell. The point I am making is that if you are not a born again believer and have committed these same sins and turned away from God, you make yourself an enemy of God. Thus, you subject yourself to God's righteous judgment and captivity.

Finally, it is interesting to note that the Israelites committed seven sins. They built watchtowers and fortified cities, sacred pillars, set up Asherim, served idols, stiffened their necks, rejected God's statutes and commands, and became vain, chasing vanity and becoming like the world.

Seven is the number of completion. The cycle of sin was complete. The nation of Israel made themselves enemies of God and God had had enough! Justice must be served. I recognized the same parallels in my own life. I made myself an enemy to God and justice must be served.

CHAPTER 13

B ecause of their sins, God caused the King of Assyria, Shalmaneser, to take Israel captive. Like the nation of Israel, my sins required justice so I was taken captive (incarcerated). Israel's captivity had a purpose but it was also the people's choice of how they would live in their captivity.

Would they live in the futility of their captivity – angry, stubbornly defiant, rejecting God? Would I live that same life? Will you live that way? Your time in captivity (incarcerated) can be redeemed to be productive and proactive to produce blessing. *"Thus says the Lord of hosts, the God of Israel, to all the exiles whom I have sent into exile from Jerusalem to Babylon, build houses and live in them, plant and eat the produce. Take wives and become the fathers of sons and daughters, and take wives for your sons and give your daughters to husbands, that they may bear sons and daughters and multiply there and not decrease."*
- Jeremiah 29:4-6

In other words, God wants to bless you even in your captivity, incarceration, or circumstances. In the midst of your trials, live and act as though God is still God.

Take, for example, the story of Elisha the prophet found in II Kings 6:8-17. The King of Syria had staged a series of raids against the cities of Israel. These raids were thwarted by

Elisha's advice to the King of Israel. This angered the Syrian King so he made plans to take Elisha captive.

The King of Syria sent horses, chariots and men to encircle the city in the middle of the night. The next morning Elisha's servant awoke and became fearful when he noticed that the entire city was compassed about by the Syrian army. Excitedly, he asked Elisha, "What shall we do?" Elisha's response surely stunned the young servant:

"Fear not: for they that be with us are more than they that be with them."

– II Kings 6:16

I can imagine the servant did exactly what most people do today when faced with dire circumstances. "Elisha! Are you crazy? The whole city is surrounded by an army!" Then Elisha calmly prayed.

". . . Lord I pray that you open his eyes that he may see. And the Lord opened the eyes of the young man; and he saw: and behold, the mountain was full of horses and chariots of God." – II Kings 6:17

You see, the servant only saw his earthly physical circumstances: they were captive in their own city. However, Elisha saw with spiritual eyes and did not fear but rather rested in his faith that God is God and would remain in sovereign control despite the dire outward circumstances. This is the same principle that God was communicating to the nation of Israel.

Next, notice that not one thing that God had commanded the captives was negative. There are many negative, criminal and detrimental activities that an inmate can engage in. One of the most pervasive is complaining. The complaining is constant in prison and if you fail to guard your heart and tongue, it is an easy trap to fall into.

Do not misunderstand, there is a LOT to complain about in prison or in life in general, but ask yourself: will my complaining bring glory to God? Will it advance the cause of Christ? How will it affect my testimony to those around me?

The Bible is replete with examples of complaining and murmuring. They all have serious, even disastrous results for the person or people doing the complaining. Remember, complaining is a choice.

In the scientific field of physics there is a familiar law that states that for every action there is an equal and opposite reaction. This is also a spiritual law. Righteous, holy God does not tolerate complaining. Complaining shows a lack of faith, a lack of thanksgiving, and fear.

During the exodus from Egypt, the nation of Israel complained on eleven separate occasions. It began with complaining about Pharaoh's army (Exodus 14:1-31), bitter waters (Exodus 15:22-27), lack of food (Exodus 16:1-36), lack of water (Exodus 7:1-7), the hardships of desert life (Numbers 11:1-3), lack of meat (Numbers 11:4-35), the size and power of those living in the land (Numbers 14:1-35), the authority and leadership of Moses and Aaron (Numbers 16:1-35), killing Korah and those who rebelled with him (Numbers 16:41-50), lack of water . . . again (Numbers 20:1-43), and manna, and being brought into the desert (Numbers 21:4-9).

Next, look what God said:

"Seek the welfare of the city where I have sent you into exile, and pray to the Lord on its behalf, for in its welfare you will have welfare." –
Jeremiah 29:7

Incredible! Is God instructing us to pray for our captors, i.e., the prison, the C/Os and the administration? That is precisely what He wants you to do.

"By the blessing of the upright (you) a city is exalted, but by the mouth of the wicked it is torn down." – Proverbs 11:11

"First of all, then, I urge that entreaties and prayers, petitions, and

thanksgivings be made on behalf of all men, for kings and all who are in authority, so that we may lead a tranquil and quiet life in all godliness and dignity." — I Timothy 2:1-2

You have a choice to complain or pray. Both will produce results. It seems like the more complaining that takes place the worse things get. The same principle applies for your job. You could be the cause of the company's decline, layoffs, or even losing your own job. Your welfare and that of your co-workers is inextricably linked to the welfare of your employer.

Earlier I mentioned that every action has an equal and opposite reaction. In the Bible, this is known as the "command-reward" or "if-then" principle. God commanded the captives to build houses, dwell in them, plant gardens and eat from them, take wives and have sons and daughters, take wives for their sons and give daughters to husbands, and pray for and seek peace for the city and their captors.

What would be their reward?

"For I know the thoughts that I think toward you, says the Lord, thoughts of peace, and not of evil, to give you an expected end. Then you shall call upon me and you shall pray unto me, and I will hear you, And you will seek me and find me when you search with all your heart. And I will be found of you, and I will turn away your captivity, and I will gather you from all nations and from all places where I have driven you, and I will bring you again into the place where I caused you to be carried away captive."
— Jeremiah 29:11-14

All that the captives had to do was obey the commands to receive the reward. This principle is further illustrated in the book of Proverbs.

COMMAND: *"Trust in the Lord with all your heart; and lean not on your own understanding. In all your ways acknowledge God."*

REWARD: *"and He will direct your paths." — Proverbs 3:5-6*

COMMAND: *"Be not wise in your own eyes: fear the Lord and depart from evil."*

REWARD: *"It shall be health to your navel, and marrow to your bones."*

— *Proverbs 3:7-8*

COMMAND: *"Honor the Lord with your substance and with the firstfruits of all your increase."*

REWARD: *"So shall your barns be filled with abundance and your presses shall burst with new wine." — Proverbs 3:9-10*

COMMAND: *"My son, despise not the chastening of the Lord, do not be weary of His correction."*

REWARD: *"For whoever the Lord loves He corrects, even as a father corrects the son who he loves." — Proverbs 3:11-12*

COMMAND: *"My son, let not my words depart from you. Keep sound wisdom and discretion."*

REWARD: *"They shall be life unto you soul, and grace to your neck. Then you will walk in the way safely, and your foot will not stumble." — Proverbs 3:21-23*

Wherever you are, whatever your situation or circumstance you find yourself in, obey God's commands for you and have faith that God is truly God. It may seem dark and there is no way out of your situation. Know for certainty that not only is He THE way but he can make A way. Listen to His voice, obey what he is telling you to do, and then reap the rewards of His faithful blessings.

Your case, crime, circumstance or situation does not mean that God cannot or will not use you. He can and will if you allow Him to do so. You have a purpose and He has a plan. Your purpose is not dependent on your position but your position has a purpose in His plan, and your past does not preclude your purpose.

CHAPTER 14

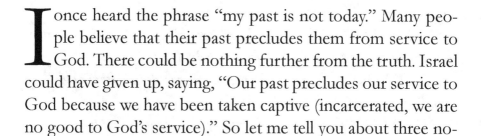

I once heard the phrase "my past is not today." Many people believe that their past precludes them from service to God. There could be nothing further from the truth. Israel could have given up, saying, "Our past precludes our service to God because we have been taken captive (incarcerated, we are no good to God's service)." So let me tell you about three notorious men, convicted murderers who God chose and called in His service

The first man had a strike against him even before he was born. He should have been aborted. He was born incarcerated. You see, both his mother and father were incarcerated as political prisoners at the time of his birth.

However, by the grace of God, the child was adopted into a very wealthy and powerfully influential family. He was raised in the finest homes, educated in the best schools and wealthy beyond measure. He wanted for nothing. The man became an engineer and eventually a city planner. By all accounts, he was incredibly successful and his future held even more promise.

As an adult, he learned of the story of his birth parents and his own racial heritage. His parents had been incarcerated for over 40 years. Upon hearing the story of his family history, something in him changed and he soon became like the rest of his family, incarcerated. He threw away his future of wealth, power, easy living, notoriety, and success.

During his incarceration, he witnessed many abuses and unfair treatment of other incarcerated people. The anger and resentment built up over time. He was repressing his feelings like a smoldering volcano. All the while, the pressure continued to build.

Then one day he witnessed an incident that caused his anger to violently erupt and he killed an officer. He became fearful, escaped captivity and was on the run for 40 years before he was apprehended. He was then 80 years old but God had a great plan and purpose for him despite his age, his case, and his past.

The second man also came from humble beginnings. He was the youngest of eight children born into a God-fearing family. Not only was he the youngest child but he was a runt with red hair. You know, his older siblings picked and teased him mercilessly. This is probably the etiology of his "short man" complex. For all intents and purposes, it appeared he grew up in a great home with a middle class background. He was very confident, self-aware, and self assured.

As a child, he was homeschooled but it was during a time when education did not mean as much as it does today. He was most comfortable outdoors taking care of the family's livestock. He was also an accomplished, self-taught musician. His future was not as bright as the first man but he knew he could make a middle class living by working hard.

Then one day a stranger showed up at the family home and offered this "runt" in the family an internship. The internship would be with a successful and powerful leader with the promise that he would become the chief executive himself one day. Soon after, this juvenile came upon an incident of bullying.

The bully was much greater in size than all the others around him. The boy's "short man complex" must have stirred up his anger and with premeditation he murdered the much larger bully.

As a juvenile, this act did not stop the young man from achieving success. Eventually, he went on to complete the internship that he had been selected for. Years later, as promised, he was thrust into the leadership role where he became rich and powerful.

Though he was a spiritual man, he had a few character flaws and was subject to the same temptations of all men. He met a beautiful young lady who was married. He seduced her. When she informed him of her pregnancy he panicked knowing she was married. This scandal would surely bring about retribution from her husband. However, far more worrisome was he of the scandal that this leader, this pillar of society would be labeled an adulterer. There had to be a cover-up.

There were two attempts to cover up the adulterous affair. Both attempts failed. Once again, with premeditation he devised a plan to have the husband killed. His intent was to commit murder.

Though he did not physically kill the husband, he had committed adultery and planned the murder. The man was caught and found guilty under the theory of accountability. This man who rose to power from humble beginnings, murdered a man as a juvenile, committed adultery, and murdered his lover's husband. He could have given up. But God did not give up on him and had a great plan and purpose for his life.

The third man came from a well-to-do family of multinational citizenship. The family business was manufactured homes. He was well educated, especially in the areas of law, religion and philosophy. His education caused him to be arrogant and judgmental of others.

This man was considered to be an "intellectual elite" and as such, he was an agnostic. Not only was he an agnostic but he was a militant agnostic who blasphemed God and persecuted anyone who demonstrated any outward display of faith and spirituality. If anyone challenged him intellectually in spiritual matters, he became a violent aggressor. In other words, he became a bully.

The fact of the matter is that this was false bravado to compensate for the spiritual truths that he so readily knew from his privileged education. This man was actually a follower.

This man never actually killed anyone but he was a part of several mob actions where many people were assaulted and killed, mainly Christians. He was eventually apprehended and convicted of assault and battery, mob action, and murder under the theory of accountability. Despite his past and his hatred for all things pertaining to God, God had a great plan and purpose for his life.

Who were these murderous men? How could and why would God use men like this? They are Moses, King David, and the apostle Paul. Moses became God's chosen leader to lead the nation of Israel out of exile. He went on to become a prolific author, writing the first five books of the Bible.

David became king of Israel, a great military leader. He penned 73 Psalms. David is mentioned in the direct line of genealogy of Jesus.

Paul became the most prolific evangelist of his time, as well as writer of almost two-thirds of the New Testament.

After these men were caught in their murderous lifestyles, they were sentenced to a life of service to God. Once sentenced, they all had one thing in common: they had an earnest expectation and hope in God that they would be used mightily in service for the kingdom of heaven.

The point of using these three men as examples is to prove that no matter what your age, crime, circumstance, or status or your incarceration, God says your past is not today. You may be a product of your past but you do not have to remain a prisoner to it.

Understand! When God calls you into His family, into His service, He does not constantly remind you of your past, your crimes, or sins. When you are born into the family of God you are made new.

"Therefore if anyone is in Christ, he is a new creature; the old things are passed away, behold all things are new." – II Corinthians 5:17

It has been said that God discards our sins into the sea of forgetfulness. Why then are you constantly launching your row boat of condemnation to go fishing for your past? Stop being a prisoner to your past. It is time to let the past go once and for all. Embrace what the future holds for you.

"Cease striving and know that I am God." –Psalm 46:10

Do not turn around and look at your past. This is exactly what Lot's wife did in the book of Genesis.

"But his wife looked back and she became a pillar of salt." – Genesis 19:26

She looked back at the past, the sins and sinful lifestyle that she loved. However, the past enticed her more than the future. If you look back you will be staring at sin, death, and defeat. Always look forward to righteousness, life and victory.

Define your future. Do not let your past define who you are today. God has a great plan and purpose for your life. Like Moses, David, and Paul embrace the expected hope that God can and will use you where you are now.

CHAPTER 15

A great boxer of his time, Mike Tyson was told by a reporter that his opponent had a great plan to defeat the heavyweight champion. Mike Tyson replied, "Everyone has a plan until he gets punched in the face." The captive nation had a plan.

". . . it's hopeless (captivity)! For we are going to follow our own plans and each of us will act according to the stubbornness of his evil heart."
— Jeremiah 18:12

Moses' plan was to be a husband, father, and shepherd. David's plan was to be a middleclass shepherd, and Paul's plan was to thwart the spread of Christianity. They never anticipated the call of God on their lives, His plan and His purpose.

You see, man is unique in that God has given us freewill. Most of the time we exploit this liberty to establish plans of our own lives without asking our sovereign Creator what His plan and purpose for our life may be.

"Every man's way is right in his own eyes, but the Lord weighs the hearts."
— Proverbs 21:2

We make our own plan and then begin to pray, asking God to bless our plan. When our plan does not come to fruition, we become disappointed and angry. However, God has something to say about our plans.

"Devise a plan, but it will be thwarted; state a proposal but it will not stand."

– Isaiah 8:10

As I stated in an earlier chapter, I was a planner to the highest degree, almost to the point of obsessive-compulsive. I had a daily, weekly, monthly, and yearly plan. Any deviation brought about disappointment and anger: disappointment in myself that I had failed to recognize a potential flaw in my plan and anger at anyone who had caused the deviation, including God. Now, do not get me wrong. I know there is this thing called "life" and life has a funny way of changing plans.

I had great plans to be a husband, father, and doctor. I knew at a very young age that I wanted and would be a husband and father in accordance with His will and plan. Becoming a doctor was my will and my plan.

I reflect on being a husband, I am reminded of how God thwarted my plans. When I enlisted in the United States Air Force, the Air Force recruited from within for its special forces knows as "pararescue" or "pj" and "combat control." This would be an exciting challenge and career field.

Upon completion of basic training and pararescue q-school (qualification school) you would be placed in the "training pipeline." This consisted of training at several different military installations in different specialties, such as S.C.U.B.A., parachuting, medical E.M.T., etc.

The training pipeline was two and a half to three years. I knew I wanted to be married and start a family, and three years of moving around every few months along with rigorous special forces training would not be conducive to any relationship. I just knew in my heart that my bride was waiting to be found.

In December of 1988 I was stationed at Clark Air Base in

the Philippines. A month later, January 1989, I was assigned as a sponsor to a new incoming airman to our squadron. I made plans to show him around the base and go out on the town. He asked if he could bring a young lady from another squadron who did not yet have a sponsor. They had traveled together on the journey from the U.S. to the Philippines. I agreed.

Later that night there was a knock on my door and I opened it, welcoming the two "newbies" in. There stood before me a beautiful gift. My bride to be! Jimmy introduced us and without saying so much as hi, hello or how are you, I blurted out loud, "I'm going to marry you one of these days." It came out involuntarily, word vomit. I had known this girl for literally seven seconds when I told her I was going to marry her. Later, I found out that she thought that it was a "creepy" thing to say. However, we became inseparable.

It turned out that both of us had lived in the same city in Oklahoma. I ate at the restaurant where she waitressed. In fact, I sat in the station she serviced, yet we both had no recollection of ever meeting.

Dawn ended up moving back to her hometown of Danville, Illinois where she enlisted in the Air Force. I moved back to Texas where I eventually enlisted in the Air Force, also. Now, some 10,000 miles from Oklahoma, we finally met in the Philippines. Truly, it was love at first sight for me. Not so much for her but as I said, we were inseparable spending every waking hour with each other. I knew for a certainty that she would be my bride. That day came exactly six months to the day after we met. Thank God for His plan and His purpose.

God's "plan-purpose" principle is the same for those who are incarcerated. Upon incarceration, I began planning how to use the law and the courts to obtain my freedom. I immersed myself in every aspect of criminal law. Eventually, I completed my paralegal certification. I was a "jailhouse lawyer," researching issues, preparing motions and briefs, and with great eloquence I could argue pro se before the court.

A judge once remarked, "It is obvious that you have educated yourself in the law remarkably well. I have spoken with the State's Attorney and the Public Defender. Both agree that, if not for your incarceration, you would be a valuable asset to either team." My plan seemed to be working. The years of mind numbing legal studies, research, and preparation were seemingly coming to fruition.

Eighteen years into my incarceration and not a single plan has produced a ruling in my favor. Why? God's plan is to trust God. I was trusting in my own abilities and plans without asking God what He wanted. Then I read:

"Give us help from trouble: for vain is the help of man. Through God we shall do valiantly: for it is God that shall tread down our enemies."
– Psalms 60:11-12

God has greater plans for us than we could ever imagine. Let's look at the story of Lazarus found in the book of John, chapter 11. Jesus received word that his friend Lazarus was sick and Jesus was needed urgently to come heal him. Jesus remarked:

"This sickness is not to end in death, but for the glory of God, so that the Son of God may be glorified by it." – John 11:4

So Jesus waited four days before traveling to Lazarus in Bethany. There he found Mary and Martha mourning the death of their brother Lazarus. Martha in her grief cried out:

"Lord, if You had been here, my brother would not have died."
– John 11:21

They led Jesus to the tomb where they had laid Lazarus. Jesus said, "Open it up." Surely startled, Martha remarked, "Lord, he's been dead four days now. Surely he stinks," meaning the body of Lazarus had begun to process of decay. It is interesting to note that the Pharisees believed it took three days for the soul to leave the body, proving you were truly dead.

After four days in the tomb Lazarus was beyond dead. Yet, Jesus looked to heaven, said a prayer and cried out, "Lazarus! Come forth!" The Bible says:

"The man who had died came forth." – John 11:44

I began to meditate on this story when I received a revelation. I was working on my own plan for what I wanted using my own efforts to utilize the law and courts to obtain my release from prison. Like Martha I did not know the plan. Martha wanted a healing while Jesus wanted a resurrection. I realized that I was going about things the wrong way. I was trying to obtain a judgment in my favor and God's greater plan was to give me mercy.

"Mercy rejoices against judgment."

or

"Mercy triumphs over judgment"
James 2:13

Judgment is the result of the law, a legal declaration whereas mercy is the result of grace. Though I was given judgment of "natural life" I now understood that it would be God's mercy that would overcome the judgment.

Another example of God's "plan-purpose" principle came unexpectedly. The Illinois Department of Corrections was closing down an entire cell house in another prison that held roughly 800 inmates. The building was being condemned as unsafe, unsanitary, and unfit for human habitation. They had to move the inmates to other facilities. To make room, the other maximum security facilities would have to send their "long term" inmates to medium security facilities.

I jumped on this opportunity (without praying and seeking

God's plan). I can be impetuous at times. Knowing my record and having no disciplinary history while incarcerated, I knew I was a shoo-in for one of the coveted slots for transfer to a medium security facility. However, my transfer never came through. Guys with disciplinary histories, trips to segregation (the hole) and gang activity were getting transferred.

A Christian brother came to me one day and said, "Do not get frustrated if you do not go." Oh, no! That means God had a different plan. "Come on, Lord! What could be better than a transfer to a medium camp?"

Later, I was disappointed to learn that my transfer request to a specific facility was denied. Now, I would have to wait six months before requesting another transfer. The next day the Assistant Warden, who had been my counselor before he was promoted to Assistant Warden, came into the law library where I was working as a paralegal and offered to send me to the medium security unit (MSU) called "The Hill." He explained that he was the one who denied my transfer because he thought my particular skills could be best utilized at MSU.

A few weeks later I was, in fact, transferred. I would be teaching, facilitating, and mentoring other men who would soon be released. I wanted a transfer to a specific facility and God's plan was to extend His favor to me to that His glory could be revealed. His plan and purpose was being worked out in my life.

CHAPTER 16

The plans and purposes of God are not always easily understood. A lot of the time they involve heartbreaking pain. Pain is the best teacher. Touch something hot and the immediate and involuntary reaction is to pull away. When our hearts are broken or we are at our lowest we become more receptive to God's teaching. I have had many teachers, instructors, and professors in my life. The greatest lesson I have learned about my relationship with God was in the aftermath of my incarceration. How could God let this happen to me, His child? I learned that the only thing worse than going through this was going through it without God. I learned to cling to God knowing He is faithful to give me what I need to endure.

I had lost everything, literally. However, I gained valuable wisdom and understanding, especially through the Psalms and Proverbs. The Book of Psalms has 150 chapters and the Book of Proverbs has 31 chapters. Each morning I would read five chapters of Psalms and one chapter of Proverbs. This meant that I could get through both books in thirty days.

The words came alive and penetrated deep into my heart and mind, proving to be great comfort when I needed it the most. There were days when I struggled to live in a Christ-like manner. As those dark days came and went, I began to internalize the negative perceptions and doubted my God's plan and purpose for my life. Once again, I questioned, "God, why don't You intervene?"

Nothing seemed to work. God was not responding in the way I thought would remedy my situation. The only option was to continue to cling to Him to change the laws and hearts of my captors.

When Joseph was at the bottom of the well waiting to be killed or sold into slavery, surely he prayed for God's intervention. No response was forthcoming. When Job experienced multiple tragedies he cried out to God for understanding. He simply did not understand the loss of his wealth, his family, and his health. Ultimately, God challenged Job to let go of his desire to know and to simply know God by trusting Him.

During this time of deep struggle, I began to learn to trust God. I could not understand why he allowed this terrible crime to happen. What I do know is that what I lost cannot be compared to what I gained. I learned to pray deeper and richer than ever before, and I learned to accept the loving embrace of God. I learned that despite the external chaos of prison life with all of its turmoil, I could have internal peace, a peace that surpasses all earthly understanding.

Inevitably, our questions of God will always remain. We are human with feeling and emotions. We want to have every heartbreak, struggle, and low point wrapped up in a neat little bow. However, we have to accept that we are not God and He is. His ways will always be above our ways and we should learn to be content in every circumstance. As the apostle Paul points out:

"Not that I speak in respect of want: for I have learned, in whatsoever state I am, therewith to be content: I know both how to be abased, and I

know how to abound: everywhere and in all things I am instructed to be both full and to be hungry, both to about and to suffer need." – Philippians 4:11-12

When you struggle with the hurts and pains of this world, rest confidently knowing that God gave His son Jesus to come to earth as an example of how to survive in this cruel world as an instrument of His love.

Always remember, Jesus was a convicted felon sentenced to the death penalty. He was rejected, abused and ultimately crucified. He alone understands the pain we experience as convicts. His example provided a template of how we are to live and triumph in a broken world. We are not exempt from the hurts, pains, and struggles of this life. In fact, he gave us the gift of His Holy Spirit to be our comforter, counselor, and guide. When we are too downtrodden to lift our eyes or voice to heaven, the Holy Spirit prays for us. God is faithful and hears our prayers even in our incarceration.

Stop and think about the many convicts in the Bible. There was Moses the murderer, Joseph the convicted (but innocent) rapist, Daniel the usurper, sentenced to death by being thrown into the lions' den. There was Shadrach, Meshach, and Abednego the stubbornly defiant children sentenced to death in the fiery furnace. Next, there was the arrogant, prideful Samson convicted of - well, arrogance, pride and anarchy. The prophet Ezekiel committed no crime but was nonetheless taken captive as a part of God's plan and purpose for his life. King David was a murderer and adulterer. Almost all of the apostles suffered at one time an incarceration. John the Baptist was incarcerated and killed for speaking the truth. The woman caught in adultery was surely to be sentenced to death by stoning before Jesus intervened. Finally, there was Jesus himself, a completely innocent man convicted and sentenced to death.

What are the two things that all of these people had in common? They were all convicted criminals yet God saw the redemptive value in their lives. Each person had a God-given plan and a God-given purpose despite their conviction, sentence or incarceration. Though the state (or feds) always take into consideration the "costs" of your incarceration, think of it as God's investment that will provide unparalleled returns for the redemptive value of your life. When you finally receive the deep, abiding truths that God loves you, you have redemptive value, and He has a great plan and purpose for your life, you can fully experience the EXPECTED HOPE.

EPILOGUE

A Personal Word From the Author

I ncarceration or being a convicted felon does not have to be the scarlet letter of your life. I have written throughout this book of the plans and purposes of God for your life. However, it is up to you to seek God's will for your life. To do so you must first become a born-again believer. If you are not a born-again believer, I'm asking you now to consider accepting Jesus Christ as your personal Lord and Savior.

If you truly desire to be different person and want to transform your life, pray this simple prayer: Dear God, I am a sinner who needs Your forgiveness. I repent of my sins. I submit my life unto You. Please forgive me. Jesus, I confess that You are the Savior of the world who died for my sins. I ask You to be my personal Lord and Savior.

If you prayed this prayer in faith you have been born-again and are now a child of the living God. It is important that you get into chapel services or a Bible based church. Read your Bible and pray daily. Ask God to reveal His plans and purposes for your life.

Finally, share this book with others. As Christians, it is our duty to share the good news or the gospel of Christ so that others may also experience salvation and EXPECTED HOPE.

EDUCATIONAL AND SELF-HELP RESOURCES

Degree Programs
Christian Bible College and Seminary
605 S.W. U.S. Highway 40, #336
Blue Springs, MO 64014

Liberty Bible College and Seminary
5480 S. Suncoast Blvd.
Homosassa, FL 34446

International College of Bible Theology
114 E. Main St.
P.O. Box 339
Norris City, IL 62869

Certificate Programs
Church of Christ
401 Fir St.
Vacaville, CA 95688

International Prison Ministry
P.O. Box 2868
Costa Mesa, CA 92628

Law and Grace Ministries
Correspondence Division
P.O. Box 562
Belleville, IL 62221

Lamp and Light Publishers
26 Road 5577
Farmington, NM 87401

College Guild

P.O. Box 6448
Brunswick, ME 04011

Criminon Illinois
P.O. Box 285
Grayslake, IL 60030

Jesus Is The Way Prison Ministry
P.O. Box 98
Rantoul, IL 61866

Global University
1211 S. Glen Stone Ave.
Springfield, MO 65804

Salvation Army
Bible Correspondence
5550 Prairie Stone Parkway
Hoffman Estates, IL 60192

Set Free Ministries of MO/IL
P.O. Box 2206
St. Louis, MO 63126

Evangel Prison Ministry
P.O. Box 19229
Louisville, KY 40259

Exodus Prison Ministry
P.O. Box 6363
Lubbock, TX 79493

Miscellaneous Resources
Light and Life Home Bible Study (Free Books)
P.O. Box 5442
Bloomington, IL 61702

Salem Church (Bible studies)
Light and Life Home Bible Study
4925 E. 1250 North Road
Gridley, IL 61744

Moody Bible Institute
Distance Learning
820 N. LaSalle Blvd.
Chicago, IL 60610

New Life Corrections Ministry
215 E. New York St.
Aurora, IL 60505

Social Security Administration
600 W. Madison St.
Chicago, IL 60661

Chicago VA Regional Office
2122 W. Taylor St.
Chicago, IL 60612